AN
OXFORD ANTHOLOGY
OF
SHAKESPEARE

AN
OXFORD ANTHOLOGY
OF
SHAKESPEARE

Selected and Introduced by
STANLEY WELLS

CLARENDON PRESS · OXFORD
1987

Oxford University Press, Walton Street, Oxford OX2 6DP

Oxford New York Toronto
Delhi Bombay Calcutta Madras Karachi
Petaling Jaya Singapore Hong Kong Tokyo
Nairobi Dar es Salaam Cape Town
Melbourne Auckland

and associated companies in
Beirut Berlin Ibadan Nicosia

Oxford is a trade mark of Oxford University Press

Published in the United States
by Oxford University Press, New York

British Library Cataloguing in Publication Data
Shakespeare, William
An Oxford anthology of Shakespeare.
I. Title II. Wells, Stanley
822.3'3 PR2768
ISBN 0–19–812935–1

Library of Congress Cataloging in Publication Data
Shakespeare, William, 1564–1616.
An Oxford anthology of Shakespeare.
Includes index.
I. Wells, Stanley W., 1930– .
PR2771.W45 1987 822.3'3 87–5788
ISBN 0–19–812935–1

Set by Wyvern Typesetting, Bristol
Printed in Great Britain
at the University Printing House, Oxford
by David Stanford
Printer to the University

FOR JESSICA
(who helped)
AND CLEMENCY
(who would have if she could have)

CONTENTS

❂

A NOTE ON THE TEXT

THE text used for this volume is that of *William Shakespeare: The Complete Works*, general editors Stanley Wells and Gary Taylor (Oxford, 1986), and act, scene, and line references are to that volume. An ellipsis (. . .) indicates that the opening of the extract does not correspond with the opening of the speech. The title given to each extract has been provided by the editor, as have the headnotes. Broken brackets (⌈ ⌉) indicate that a line or phrase is irrecoverably lost.

The sentence from Bernard Levin's *Enthusiasms* quoted on pp. xi–xii is reproduced in the US by permission of Curtis Brown Ltd., London.

INTRODUCTION

M o s t people, I suppose, regard Shakespeare as the world's greatest writer. In English-speaking countries, at least, his works have long formed the basis of a literary education. Even persons who have never read or seen one of his plays are familiar with phrases from them. As Bernard Levin puts it in one brilliant sentence:

If you cannot understand my argument, and declare 'It's Greek to me', you are quoting Shakespeare; if you claim to be more sinned against than sinning, you are quoting Shakespeare; if you recall your salad days, you are quoting Shakespeare; if you act more in sorrow than in anger, if your wish is father to the thought, if your lost property has vanished into thin air, you are quoting Shakespeare; if you have ever refused to budge an inch or suffered from green-eyed jealousy, if you have played fast and loose, if you have been tongue-tied, a tower of strength, hoodwinked or in a pickle, if you have knitted your brows, made a virtue of necessity, insisted on fair play, slept not one wink, stood on ceremony, danced attendance (on your lord and master), laughed yourself into stitches, had short shrift, cold comfort or too much of a good thing, if you have seen better days or lived in a fool's paradise—why, be that as it may, the more fool you, for it is a foregone conclusion that you are (as good luck would have it) quoting Shakespeare; if you think it is early days and clear out bag and baggage, if you think it is high time and that that is the long and short of it, if you believe that the game is up and that truth will out even if it involves your own flesh and blood, if you lie low till the crack of doom because you suspect foul play, if you have your teeth set on edge (at one fell swoop) without rhyme or reason, then—to give the devil his due—if the truth were known (for surely you have a tongue in your head) you are quoting Shakespeare; even if you bid me good riddance and send me packing, if you wish I was dead as a doornail, if you think I am an eyesore, a laughing stock, the devil incarnate, a stony-hearted villain, bloody-minded or a blinking idiot, then—by Jove! O Lord! Tut, tut! for goodness' sake! what the dickens! but me no buts—it is all one to me, for you are quoting Shakespeare. (*Enthusiasms* (1983), pp. 167–8)

Not only has much of Shakespeare's language passed into common currency, his characters, too, have become type-figures. In my boyhood, someone throwing a fit of temperament was said to be playing Hamlet; a miser is still a Shylock, a lovesick youth a Romeo: even Shakespeare's own name is apt to be applied mockingly to one suspected of harbouring aspirations to literary distinction. The notion that Shakespeare would supply a quotation suited to any aspect of human experience has long been a cliché. In his own time, extracts from his works were copied into commonplace books and printed in anthologies. The first anthology devoted entirely to Shakespeare, William Dodd's *The Beauties of Shakespeare*, appeared in 1752 and was frequently reprinted. It is made up of a number of short extracts arranged (in the first edition) under the titles of the plays from which they are taken, each supplied with a title ('Too Ambitious Love', 'Custom of Seducers', 'A Lovely Woman', 'Malicious Men', 'Hector in Battle', and the like); and there are many notes, some lengthy. It enjoyed a long-lasting success, being reprinted frequently until 1911, and then again as late as 1936. There have been many other collections, too. Some, such as *The Wisdom and Genius of Shakespeare* (1838) and *The Philosophy of Shakespeare* (1841), have presented the writer as a sage; others, such as *Religious and Moral Sentences Culled from the Works of Shakespeare Compared with Sacred Passages drawn from Holy Writ* (1843) and *Shakespeare's Morals: Suggestive Selections* (1880), as a moralist. Others have sought to be of more practical utility: they include *Shakespeare Proverbs* (1848), *Shakespeare's Household Words* (1859), and *A Casket of Jewels from Shakespeare*, subtitled *A Thought for Every Day in the Year*

(1912). Amorists have been offered *Cupid's Birthday Book: One Thousand Love Darts from Shakespeare* (1875), *The Sweet Silvery Sayings of Shakespeare on the Softer Sex. Compiled by an Old Soldier* (1877), and *The Lover's Shakespeare*, published by Gay and Bird in 1900. More specialized collections include *Shakespeare in Time of War* (1916), *Shakespeare as a Letter Writer and Artist in Prose* (1922), *The Crows of Shakespeare* (1899), and *Shakespeare on Golf, With Special Reference to St Andrews Links* (1885). In recent years the most successful anthology has been George Rylands's *The Ages of Man*, which ingeniously arranges many excerpts from Shakespeare under the three principal headings of Youth, Manhood, and Age, and which formed the basis for a recital in which Sir John Gielgud richly displayed his mastery of Shakespearian performance.

In spite of the success of these and similar collections, objection may legitimately be made to the practice of detaching sections of stage plays from their dramatic and theatrical context and presenting them—like the 'bleeding hunks of Wagner' sometimes offered in concert programmes—as if they were independent pieces meant to be read. Shakespeare is frequently praised above all for the organic unity of his works, in which every detail is seen as contributory to the overall effect, with the result that detachment of a part from the whole must diminish the quality of the part itself. And Shakespeare has increasingly come to be regarded above all as a man of the theatre, writing not dramatic poems but poetic dramas, scripts that realize themselves only in performance: writing, that is to say, dialogue that needs to be heard; building into this dialogue significant silences, and causing it to depend for its effect sometimes on the reactions of silent listeners; designing stage action that is itself part of the play's meaning, issuing inseparably from the dialogue; deepening the meaning of one scene by its juxtaposition with another; writing poetry and prose of cumulative impact, so that words and phrases are illuminated by their links with speech or action in quite other parts of the play, and the effect of no part is complete until the last words are spoken, the final silence experienced.

These are reasons, not just why Shakespeare cannot properly be enjoyed in extracts, but why he cannot be fully appreciated anywhere except in the theatre. He seems to have felt this himself; at any rate, he displayed no visible interest in the printing of his plays, and about half of them were still in manuscript when he died—in manuscript, but not unpublished, because, for Shakespeare, performance was publication, and his scripts fulfilled themselves in the collaborative and evanescent art of his interpreters.

But from early in his career the fact that his plays had much to offer to readers was acknowledged even by men of the theatre such as his friends who put together the first collected edition of his plays, only a few years after he died. John Heminges and Henry Condell took great pains, they claimed, to represent their author's plays 'cured and perfect of their limbs'; and they put the plays into print not just so that actors could go on playing them—the very format of their volume was a deterrent to its use in the theatre—but so that lovers of literature could read them: 'Read him therefore, and again, and again, and if then you do not like him, surely you are in some manifest danger not to understand him.'

This injunction has been heeded, and from early in the seventeenth century to the present there has been a divergent stream of editions of Shakespeare: those presenting the plays to be read, in a form as close to the original as convenience of reading permitted; and those presenting the plays as they were acted, or as they might be acted, in theatres at the time of printing.

Of course, Shakespeare's are not the only plays to have led a double life. Almost since the invention of printing, plays have streamed from the presses, and have found readers. But the plays of Shakespeare (and of some, but not all, of his contemporaries) have long been recognized as offering an exceptional degree of literary pleasure. At no other period in the history of the English theatre have the arts of literature and drama been so intensely interfused; at no other period has poetic drama—in the fullest sense of the term—been the dominant theatrical form. Until Shakespeare's early manhood, plays—miracles, mysteries, and interludes—were regularly written entirely in verse; but by and large it is workmanlike verse that does not burst into poetry. Not until Christopher Marlowe and Robert Greene came on the scene, around the time that Shakespeare's own career was beginning, did dramatic verse spring to poetic life. And it was not many years after Shakespeare died before prose—albeit the highly mannered, self-conscious prose of Etherege and Congreve—became the dominant vehicle of successful drama. Verse plays continued to be written; but only in Shakespeare's lifetime is the best poetry of the age to be found in the drama.

The close relationship between the arts of poetry and drama is indicated by the fact that the standard Elizabethan and Jacobean term for a maker of plays was a 'poet'. Drama of the period was heavily influenced by works written to be read. Bernard Shaw praised Shakespeare's 'gift of telling a story (provided someone else told it to him first)', and indeed almost all of the plays are based on tales that had already been told and had found literary expression. He drew on classical poets such as Ovid and Virgil; on Chaucer's *Canterbury Tales* and Spenser's *Faerie Queene*; on prose fictions such as Boccaccio's *Decameron* and Sidney's *Arcadia*; on histories such as Plutarch's *Lives of the Noble Grecians and Romans* and the English chronicles of Edward Hall and Raphael Holinshed. He refashioned already existing plays, such as Plautus' *Menaechmi* (for *The Comedy of Errors*), the anonymous *King Leir*, and George Whetstone's unacted *Promos and Cassandra* (for *Measure for*

artistic stylization lies behind even some of their simplest-seeming utterances, and is most evidently discernible in their longer speeches. However much we may subscribe to the Coleridgean view of the organic nature of Shakespeare's dramatic structures—and it is a view that modern criticism tends to exaggerate—it is undeniable that these structures are composed of other, lesser structures, just as even the most closely integrated operatic scores may draw on the forms of aria, cavatina, or rondo, waltz, polonaise, or march, chaconne, passacaglia, or fugue. In general, literary forms are not as tightly knit as musical ones, but Shakespeare's literary education would have familiarized him with conventions associated with common topics of expression, such as speeches of praise (panegyrics or encomia), blessings, curses, military and funeral orations, laments, epitaphs, and so on. Such conventions are not restricted to verse: Hamlet's prose meditations on death (pp. 370–1) are no less artfully wrought than Richard II's verse laments (p. 343), and speeches such as Falstaff's encomium on sherry (pp. 212–13), Shylock's self-justification (p. 168), or Benedick's requirements of a wife (pp. 69–70) are demonstrably the work of a writer with rhetorical training. Very small units, too, can be literary in origin: Shakespeare draws on the rich legacy of proverbs, epigrams, sententiae, apophthegms and aphorisms—'wise saws and modern instances' (p. 3)—of which numerous collections were available, sometimes providing him with the material for sparkling 'one-liners'.

These characteristics of Shakespeare's work mean that it is easy to regard parts of his plays (and even of his narrative poems) as detachable units with their own integrity, and indeed it is a valid critical procedure to examine the units of which his work is composed while also considering their relationship to the whole of which they form a part. This is more easily done in reading than in the theatre. Performance carries the mind rapidly forward. Pacing is one of Shakespeare's greatest skills, and his dramatic verse derives much of its power from its cumulative impact. 'Gallop apace, you fiery-footed steeds', says Juliet, and, though the actress would be wrong to gallop the verse, she will naturally urge it forward by the force of her simulated emotion, attempting to catch us up in her passions, her fears, not to make us linger to observe the structure of the verse. The rapt identification of a performer with the words the dramatist gives him to speak is among the highest pleasures the drama can offer, but reading to oneself has its pleasures, too, and Shakespeare's verse offers satisfaction at both levels. Indeed, he seems sometimes to have acknowledged that what he wrote was, while not necessarily below par in itself, a hindrance to the pulse of the drama. The revised text of *King Lear* (*The Tragedy of King Lear*) omits from the earlier version (*The History of King Lear*) an entire scene from which we include an extract (pp. 320–1), and some fine lines given in the first, quarto printing of *Richard II* (pp. 198–200) were omitted when the play was printed in the Folio, probably because they, too, had been cut in the theatre.

Concentration on subsidiary units invites attention to the literary background. We become more, not less, aware of Shakespeare's artistry if we know that, for example, Mercutio's characterization of a quarrelsome man (pp. 19–20) is related to the conventions of Theophrastan character writing (and we may become more conscious of the depths of Shakespeare's reading, or of his powers of intuition, if we realize too that this is an early example of a mode that, deriving from Isaac Casaubon's translation of Theophrastus published in 1592, did not become popular as an English form until well into the seventeenth century, long after Shakespeare wrote *Romeo and Juliet*). We must acknowledge the literary basis of Shakespeare's art if we recognize that Prospero's renunciation of his magical power (pp. 268–9) is closely based on a passage from Ovid's *Metamorphoses*; that the convention of the comic catechism underlies both the meditation on honour (p. 372) spoken by the character generally known as Sir John Falstaff (but originally surnamed Oldcastle) and also Dromio's description of a kitchen wench (an account that is indebted too to the traditions of geographical description found also in *Venus and Adonis*, ll. 229–40 and in other contemporary and earlier writers); that the medieval tradition of the *consolatio*, or consolation against death, is found both in *Measure for Measure* (pp. 375–6) and in the Sonnets (p. 377); that conventions of pastoral literature inform Shakespeare's kings' reflections on the burdens of the kingly state and the advantages of a simple life (pp. 259–61 and 262–3); and that Jaques's 'All the world's a stage' (from *As You Like It*; p. 3), like Menenius' fable of the belly (from *Coriolanus*; pp. 234–6), elaborates a familiar topos.

Of course, the mere isolation of these passages will not in itself convey such information; but the invitation to consider them, and others like them, as pieces in their own right may help to draw attention to their individual features. Similarly, the juxtaposition of a number of narratives from within a variety of Shakespeare's plays (pp. 299–329) may help to indicate the importance within Shakespeare's work of a speech form that is often considered undramatic.

In choosing extracts for this collection I have had in mind one simple question: What are the passages from Shakespeare that are most readable in their own right, and that suffer least from detachment from their surroundings? Not until I had selected most of the passages did I decide on headings under which to arrange them and on the order in which they should be presented. It seemed desirable to allow the passages to determine the shape of the volume rather than to select excerpts to fit a predetermined scheme. My criterion of selection inevitably emphasizes the set piece, the more highly wrought rhetorical passages of verse and prose, at the expense of more dramatically complex sequences involving interplay among a number of characters. Of course, some of

Shakespeare's greatest dramatic writing occurs in the more complex passages; but to represent Shakespeare at his greatest as a dramatist has not been my principal aim, for that, I believe, is not properly done in extracts intended primarily for reading (though suitable also for reading aloud). So you will not find in this volume such supremely Shakespearian episodes as the gulling of Malvolio (from *Twelfth Night*), Iago's tormenting of Othello, Desdemona's 'willow' song (also from *Othello*), the death of Mark Antony (from *Antony and Cleopatra*), Lady Macbeth's sleep-walking, or the awakening to life of Hermione (in *The Winter's Tale*). These are among Shakespeare's finest achievements, but they are essentially dramatic, theatrical, and so are least fairly represented apart from their context.

What I hope you *will* find is many of the finest examples of Shakespeare's work as a literary artist who chose mostly to express himself in dramatic form. He was the most protean of writers, so the range is great. In this volume's small compass we meet characters from Ancient Rome, medieval England, and Renaissance Italy, from fairyland and myth; we hear songs of love, mourning, and consolation, and we hear tales of birth and death, of courtship and marriage, of heroism and humiliation (both comic and serious), of reunion and reconciliation; we experience Shakespeare's extraordinary capacity to body forth in words the minds, hearts, and imaginations of kings and peasants, queens and sluts, fools and wise men, cynics and idealists, warriors and pageboys, statesmen and common thieves; and in incantations, orations, conversations, soliloquies, songs, sonnets, and narrations we hear quintessential expressions of admiration and vituperation, grief and joy, sarcasm and benevolence, villainy and virtue, awe and contempt, despair and triumph, fear and courage. It is unlikely that a similar selection from the works of any other writer could represent so wide a range of human experience.

People

The Ages of Man

The Duke has offered food to the starving Orlando; while Orlando
seeks his old retainer Adam, the cynical Jaques speaks.

JAQUES   All the world's a stage,
 And all the men and women merely players.
 They have their exits and their entrances,
 And one man in his time plays many parts,
 His acts being seven ages. At first the infant,
 Mewling and puking in the nurse's arms.
 Then the whining schoolboy with his satchel
 And shining morning face, creeping like snail
 Unwillingly to school. And then the lover,
 Sighing like furnace, with a woeful ballad
 Made to his mistress' eyebrow. Then, a soldier,
 Full of strange oaths, and bearded like the pard,
 Jealous in honour, sudden, and quick in quarrel,
 Seeking the bubble reputation
 Even in the cannon's mouth. And then the justice,
 In fair round belly with good capon lined,
 With eyes severe and beard of formal cut,
 Full of wise saws and modern instances;
 And so he plays his part. The sixth age shifts
 Into the lean and slippered pantaloon,
 With spectacles on nose and pouch on side,
 His youthful hose, well saved, a world too wide

For his shrunk shank, and his big, manly voice,
Turning again toward childish treble, pipes
And whistles in his sound. Last scene of all,
That ends this strange, eventful history,
Is second childishness and mere oblivion,
Sans teeth, sans eyes, sans taste, sans everything.
   Enter Orlando bearing the aged Adam
                         (*As You Like It*, 2.7.139–66)

Juliet's Infancy

Juliet's mother, Capulet's Wife, speaks with Juliet's Nurse.

CAPULET'S WIFE
  Nurse, where's my daughter? Call her forth to me.
NURSE
  Now, by my maidenhead at twelve year old,
  I bade her come. What, lamb, what, ladybird—
  God forbid—where is this girl? What, Juliet!
    Enter Juliet
JULIET How now, who calls?
NURSE Your mother.
JULIET
  Madam, I am here. What is your will?
CAPULET'S WIFE
  This is the matter.—Nurse, give leave a while.
  We must talk in secret.—Nurse, come back again.
  I have remembered me, thou's hear our counsel.
  Thou knowest my daughter's of a pretty age.
NURSE
  Faith, I can tell her age unto an hour.
CAPULET'S WIFE She's not fourteen.
NURSE I'll lay fourteen of my teeth—and yet, to my teen be it
  spoken, I have but four—she's not fourteen. How long is it
  now to Lammastide?
CAPULET'S WIFE A fortnight and odd days.

NURSE

> Even or odd, of all days in the year
> Come Lammas Eve at night shall she be fourteen.
> Susan and she—God rest all Christian souls!—
> Were of an age. Well, Susan is with God;
> She was too good for me. But, as I said,
> On Lammas Eve at night shall she be fourteen,
> That shall she, marry, I remember it well.
> 'Tis since the earthquake now eleven years,
> And she was weaned—I never shall forget it—
> Of all the days of the year upon that day,
> For I had then laid wormwood to my dug,
> Sitting in the sun under the dovehouse wall.
> My lord and you were then at Mantua.
> Nay, I do bear a brain! But, as I said,
> When it did taste the wormwood on the nipple
> Of my dug and felt it bitter, pretty fool,
> To see it tetchy and fall out wi'th' dug!
> 'Shake', quoth the dove-house! 'Twas no need, I trow,
> To bid me trudge;
> And since that time it is eleven years,
> For then she could stand high-lone. Nay, by th' rood,
> She could have run and waddled all about,
> For even the day before, she broke her brow,
> And then my husband—God be with his soul,
> A was a merry man!—took up the child.
> 'Yea,' quoth he, 'dost thou fall upon thy face?
> Thou wilt fall backward when thou hast more wit,
> Wilt thou not, Jule?' And, by my holidam,

The pretty wretch left crying and said 'Ay'.
To see now how a jest shall come about!
I warrant an I should live a thousand years
I never should forget it. 'Wilt thou not, Jule?' quoth he,
And, pretty fool, it stinted and said 'Ay'.

CAPULET'S WIFE

Enough of this. I pray thee hold thy peace.

NURSE

Yes, madam. Yet I cannot choose but laugh
To think it should leave crying and say 'Ay'.
And yet, I warrant, it had upon it brow
A bump as big as a young cock'rel's stone.
A perilous knock, and it cried bitterly.
'Yea,' quoth my husband, 'fall'st upon thy face?
Thou wilt fall backward when thou com'st to age,
Wilt thou not, Jule?' It stinted and said 'Ay'.

JULIET

And stint thou too, I pray thee, Nurse, say I.

NURSE

Peace, I have done. God mark thee to his grace,
Thou wast the prettiest babe that e'er I nursed.
An I might live to see thee married once,
I have my wish.

(Romeo and Juliet, 1.3.1–64)

Robin Goodfellow

In the forest near Athens a fairy speaks to Robin Goodfellow, the puck.

FAIRY

    Either I mistake your shape and making quite
    Or else you are that shrewd and knavish sprite
    Called Robin Goodfellow. Are not you he
    That frights the maidens of the villag'ry,
    Skim milk, and sometimes labour in the quern,
    And bootless make the breathless housewife churn,
    And sometime make the drink to bear no barm—
    Mislead night wanderers, laughing at their harm?
    Those that 'hobgoblin' call you, and 'sweet puck',
    You do their work, and they shall have good luck.
    Are not you he?

ROBIN   Thou speak'st aright;
    I am that merry wanderer of the night.
    I jest to Oberon, and make him smile
    When I a fat and bean-fed horse beguile,
    Neighing in likeness of a filly foal;
    And sometime lurk I in a gossip's bowl
    In very likeness of a roasted crab,
    And when she drinks, against her lips I bob,
    And on her withered dewlap pour the ale.
    The wisest aunt telling the saddest tale
    Sometime for three-foot stool mistaketh me;
    Then slip I from her bum. Down topples she,

And 'tailor' cries, and falls into a cough,
And then the whole choir hold their hips, and laugh,
And waxen in their mirth, and sneeze, and swear
A merrier hour was never wasted there.

(A Midsummer Night's Dream, 2.1.32–57)

A King's Sons

The old courtier Belarius speaks of Cymbeline's sons, the princes
Guiderius and Arviragus, whom he has brought up as children of
nature.

BELARIUS

. . . These boys know little they are sons to th' King,
Nor Cymbeline dreams that they are alive.
They think they are mine, and though trained up thus
  meanly
I'th' cave wherein they bow, their thoughts do hit
The roofs of palaces, and nature prompts them
In simple and low things to prince it much
Beyond the trick of others. This Polydore,
The heir of Cymbeline and Britain, who
The King his father called Guiderius—Jove,
When on my three-foot stool I sit and tell
The warlike feats I have done, his spirits fly out
Into my story: say 'Thus mine enemy fell,
And thus I set my foot on 's neck', even then
The princely blood flows in his cheek, he sweats,
Strains his young nerves, and puts himself in posture
That acts my words. The younger brother, Cadwal,
Once Arviragus, in as like a figure
Strikes life into my speech, and shows much more
His own conceiving.

(Cymbeline, 3.3.80–98)

A Kitchenmaid

Dromio of Syracuse tells his master Antipholus of a woman who has mistaken him for his twin.

DROMIO OF SYRACUSE I am an ass, I am a woman's man, and besides myself.

ANTIPHOLUS OF SYRACUSE What woman's man? And how besides thyself?

DROMIO OF SYRACUSE Marry, sir, besides myself I am due to a woman: one that claims me, one that haunts me, one that will have me.

ANTIPHOLUS OF SYRACUSE What claim lays she to thee?

DROMIO OF SYRACUSE Marry, sir, such claim as you would lay to your horse; and she would have me as a beast—not that, I being a beast, she would have me, but that she, being a very beastly creature, lays claim to me.

ANTIPHOLUS OF SYRACUSE What is she?

DROMIO OF SYRACUSE A very reverend body; ay, such a one as a man may not speak of without he say 'sir-reverence'. I have but lean luck in the match, and yet is she a wondrous fat marriage.

ANTIPHOLUS OF SYRACUSE How dost thou mean, a fat marriage?

DROMIO OF SYRACUSE Marry, sir, she's the kitchen wench, and all grease; and I know not what use to put her to but to make a lamp of her, and run from her by her own light. I warrant her rags and the tallow in them will burn a Poland winter. If she lives till doomsday, she'll burn a week longer than the whole world.

ANTIPHOLUS OF SYRACUSE What complexion is she of?

DROMIO OF SYRACUSE Swart like my shoe, but her face nothing like so clean kept. For why?—She sweats a man may go overshoes in the grime of it.

ANTIPHOLUS OF SYRACUSE That's a fault that water will mend.

DROMIO OF SYRACUSE No, sir, 'tis in grain. Noah's flood could not do it.

ANTIPHOLUS OF SYRACUSE What's her name?

DROMIO OF SYRACUSE Nell, sir. But her name and three-quarters—that's an ell and three-quarters—will not measure her from hip to hip.

ANTIPHOLUS OF SYRACUSE Then she bears some breadth?

DROMIO OF SYRACUSE No longer from head to foot than from hip to hip. She is spherical, like a globe. I could find out countries in her.

ANTIPHOLUS OF SYRACUSE In what part of her body stands Ireland?

DROMIO OF SYRACUSE Marry, sir, in her buttocks. I found it out by the bogs.

ANTIPHOLUS OF SYRACUSE Where Scotland?

DROMIO OF SYRACUSE I found it by the barrenness, hard in the palm of her hand.

ANTIPHOLUS OF SYRACUSE Where France?

DROMIO OF SYRACUSE In her forehead, armed and reverted, making war against her heir.

ANTIPHOLUS OF SYRACUSE Where England?

DROMIO OF SYRACUSE I looked for the chalky cliffs, but I
could find no whiteness in them. But I guess it stood in her
chin, by the salt rheum that ran between France and it.

ANTIPHOLUS OF SYRACUSE Where Spain?

DROMIO OF SYRACUSE Faith, I saw it not, but I felt it hot in
her breath.

ANTIPHOLUS OF SYRACUSE Where America, the Indies?

DROMIO OF SYRACUSE O, sir, upon her nose, all o'er embel-
lished with rubies, carbuncles, sapphires, declining their
rich aspect to the hot breath of Spain, who sent whole
armadas of carracks to be ballast at her nose.

ANTIPHOLUS OF SYRACUSE Where stood Belgia, the
Netherlands?

DROMIO OF SYRACUSE O, sir, I did not look so low.

(The Comedy of Errors, 3.2.77–144)

Silvia

Who is Silvia? What is she,
   That all our swains commend her?
Holy, fair, and wise is she.
   The heaven such grace did lend her
That she might admirèd be.

Is she kind as she is fair?
   For beauty lives with kindness.
Love doth to her eyes repair
   To help him of his blindness,
And, being helped, inhabits there.

Then to Silvia let us sing
   That Silvia is excelling.
She excels each mortal thing
   Upon the dull earth dwelling.
To her let us garlands bring.
   (The Two Gentlemen of Verona, 4.2.38–52)

The Indian Boy's Mother

Oberon, King of the Fairies, has told his estranged queen, Titania, that their dissension will come to an end if she will part with 'a little changeling boy' whom Oberon desires as his henchman; Titania replies.

TITANIA   Set your heart at rest.
   The fairyland buys not the child of me.
   His mother was a vot'ress of my order,
   And in the spicèd Indian air by night
   Full often hath she gossiped by my side,
   And sat with me on Neptune's yellow sands,
   Marking th'embarkèd traders on the flood,
   When we have laughed to see the sails conceive
   And grow big-bellied with the wanton wind,
   Which she with pretty and with swimming gait
   Following, her womb then rich with my young squire,
   Would imitate, and sail upon the land
   To fetch me trifles, and return again
   As from a voyage, rich with merchandise.
   But she, being mortal, of that boy did die;
   And for her sake do I rear up her boy;
   And for her sake I will not part with him.
                    (*A Midsummer Night's Dream*, 2.1.121–37)

A Popinjay

Hotspur denies the accusation that he has refused to hand over to the King (Henry IV) prisoners taken in battle.

HOTSPUR

My liege, I did deny no prisoners;
But I remember, when the fight was done,
When I was dry with rage and extreme toil,
Breathless and faint, leaning upon my sword,
Came there a certain lord, neat and trimly dressed,
Fresh as a bridegroom, and his chin, new-reaped,
Showed like a stubble-land at harvest-home.
He was perfumèd like a milliner,
And 'twixt his finger and his thumb he held
A pouncet-box, which ever and anon
He gave his nose and took't away again—
Who therewith angry, when it next came there
Took it in snuff—and still he smiled and talked;
And as the soldiers bore dead bodies by,
He called them untaught knaves, unmannerly
To bring a slovenly unhandsome corpse
Betwixt the wind and his nobility.
With many holiday and lady terms
He questioned me; amongst the rest demanded
My prisoners in your majesty's behalf.
I then, all smarting with my wounds being cold—

To be so pestered with a popinjay!—
Out of my grief and my impatience
Answered neglectingly, I know not what—
He should, or should not—for he made me mad
To see him shine so brisk, and smell so sweet,
And talk so like a waiting gentlewoman
Of guns, and drums, and wounds, God save the mark!
And telling me the sovereign'st thing on earth
Was parmacity for an inward bruise,
And that it was great pity, so it was,
This villainous saltpetre should be digged
Out of the bowels of the harmless earth,
Which many a good tall fellow had destroyed
So cowardly, and but for these vile guns
He would himself have been a soldier.

(*1 Henry IV*, 1.3.28–63)

A Ladies' Man

Biron speaks of the French Princess's attendant, Lord Boyet.

BIRON

> This fellow pecks up wit as pigeons peas,
> And utters it again when God doth please.
> He is wit's pedlar, and retails his wares
> At wakes and wassails, meetings, markets, fairs.
> And we that sell by gross, the Lord doth know,
> Have not the grace to grace it with such show.
> This gallant pins the wenches on his sleeve.
> Had he been Adam, he had tempted Eve.
> A can carve too, and lisp, why, this is he
> That kissed his hand away in courtesy.
> This is the ape of form, Monsieur the Nice,
> That when he plays at tables chides the dice
> In honourable terms. Nay, he can sing
> A mean most meanly, and in ushering
> Mend him who can. The ladies call him sweet.
> The stairs as he treads on them kiss his feet.
> This is the flower that smiles on everyone
> To show his teeth as white as whalës bone,
> And consciences that will not die in debt
> Pay him the due of 'honey-tongued' Boyet.
>
> *(Love's Labour's Lost, 5.2.316–35)*

A Quarrelsome Man

Benvolio, Romeo's cousin, has advised Mercutio to steer clear of the Capulets for fear of a brawl.

MERCUTIO Thou art like one of these fellows that, when he enters the confines of a tavern, claps me his sword upon the table and says 'God send me no need of thee', and by the operation of the second cup, draws him on the drawer when indeed there is no need.

BENVOLIO Am I like such a fellow?

MERCUTIO Come, come, thou art as hot a jack in thy mood as any in Italy, and as soon moved to be moody, and as soon moody to be moved.

BENVOLIO And what to?

MERCUTIO Nay, an there were two such, we should have none shortly, for one would kill the other. Thou—why, thou wilt quarrel with a man that hath a hair more or a hair less in his beard than thou hast. Thou wilt quarrel with a man for cracking nuts, having no other reason but because thou hast hazel eyes. What eye but such an eye would spy out such a quarrel? Thy head is as full of quarrels as an egg is full of meat, and yet thy head hath been beaten as addle as an egg for quarrelling. Thou hast quarrelled with a man for coughing in the street because he hath wakened thy dog that hath lain asleep in the sun. Didst thou not fall out with a tailor for wearing his new doublet before Easter; with

another for tying his new shoes with old ribbon? And yet
thou wilt tutor me from quarrelling!

(Romeo and Juliet, 3.1.5–29)

A Sleeping Beauty

*Giacomo, seeking evidence with which to trick Innogen's husband into
believing that he has seduced her, has had himself smuggled into the
room where she lies asleep.*

GIACOMO

    The crickets sing, and man's o'er-laboured sense
    Repairs itself by rest. Our Tarquin thus
    Did softly press the rushes ere he wakened
    The chastity he wounded. Cytherea,
    How bravely thou becom'st thy bed! Fresh lily,
    And whiter than the sheets! That I might touch,
    But kiss, one kiss! Rubies unparagoned,
    How dearly they do't! 'Tis her breathing that
    Perfumes the chamber thus. The flame o'th' taper
    Bows toward her, and would underpeep her lids,
    To see th'enclosèd lights, now canopied
    Under these windows, white and azure-laced
    With blue of heaven's own tinct. But my design—
    To note the chamber. I will write all down.
       He writes in his tables
    Such and such pictures, there the window, such
    Th'adornment of her bed, the arras, figures,
    Why, such and such; and the contents o'th' story.
    Ah, but some natural notes about her body
    Above ten thousand meaner movables

Would testify t'enrich mine inventory.
O sleep, thou ape of death, lie dull upon her,
And be her sense but as a monument
Thus in a chapel lying. Come off, come off;
As slippery as the Gordian knot was hard.

He takes the bracelet from Innogen's arm
'Tis mine, and this will witness outwardly,
As strongly as the conscience does within,
To th' madding of her lord. On her left breast
A mole, cinque-spotted, like the crimson drops
I'th' bottom of a cowslip. Here's a voucher
Stronger than ever law could make. This secret
Will force him think I have picked the lock and ta'en
The treasure of her honour. No more. To what end?
Why should I write this down that's riveted,
Screwed to my memory? She hath been reading late,
The tale of Tereus. Here the leaf's turned down
Where Philomel gave up. I have enough.
To th' trunk again, and shut the spring of it.
Swift, swift, you dragons of the night, that dawning
May bare the raven's eye! I lodge in fear.
Though this' a heavenly angel, hell is here.

Clock strikes
One, two, three. Time, time!

(Cymbeline, 2.2.11–51)

Justice Shallow

Sir John Falstaff speaks of his old friend Justice Shallow, whom he has re-encountered after many years.

SIR JOHN . . . I do see the bottom of Justice Shallow. Lord, Lord, how subject we old men are to this vice of lying! This same starved justice hath done nothing but prate to me of the wildness of his youth and the feats he hath done about Turnbull Street; and every third word a lie, duer paid to the hearer than the Turk's tribute. I do remember him at Clement's Inn, like a man made after supper of a cheese paring. When a was naked, he was for all the world like a forked radish, with a head fantastically carved upon it with a knife. A was so forlorn that his dimensions, to any thick sight, were invisible. A was the very genius of famine. And now is this Vice's dagger become a squire, and talks as familiarly of John o' Gaunt as if he had been sworn brother to him, and I'll be sworn a ne'er saw him but once, in the Tilt-yard, and then he burst his head for crowding among the marshal's men. I saw it, and told John o' Gaunt he beat his own name; for you might have trussed him and all his apparel into an eel-skin. The case of a treble hautboy was a mansion for him, a court. And now has he land and beeves. Well, I'll be acquainted with him if I return; and't shall go hard but I'll make him a philosopher's two stones to me. If the young dace be a bait for the old pike, I see no reason in the law of nature but I may snap at him. Let time shape, and there an end.

(2 *Henry IV*, 3.2.297–323)

Richard of Gloucester

Edward, Duke of York, has become King Edward IV; his brother, the hunchback Richard of Gloucester, is ambitious for the throne.

RICHARD GLOUCESTER

Now is the winter of our discontent
Made glorious summer by this son of York;
And all the clouds that loured upon our house
In the deep bosom of the ocean buried.
Now are our brows bound with victorious wreaths,
Our bruisèd arms hung up for monuments,
Our stern alarums changed to merry meetings,
Our dreadful marches to delightful measures.
Grim-visaged war hath smoothed his wrinkled front,
And now—instead of mounting barbèd steeds
To fright the souls of fearful adversaries—
He capers nimbly in a lady's chamber
To the lascivious pleasing of a lute.
But I, that am not shaped for sportive tricks
Nor made to court an amorous looking-glass,
I that am rudely stamped and want love's majesty
To strut before a wanton ambling nymph,
I that am curtailed of this fair proportion,
Cheated of feature by dissembling nature,
Deformed, unfinished, sent before my time
Into this breathing world scarce half made up—

And that so lamely and unfashionable
That dogs bark at me as I halt by them—
Why, I in this weak piping time of peace
Have no delight to pass away the time,
Unless to spy my shadow in the sun
And descant on mine own deformity.
And therefore since I cannot prove a lover
To entertain these fair well-spoken days,
I am determinèd to prove a villain
And hate the idle pleasures of these days.

(Richard III, 1.1.1–31)

Henry Bolingbroke and King Richard II

King Henry IV (Henry Bolingbroke), distressed that his son Prince Harry spends too much time with 'vulgar company', explains how he retained his own dignity while Richard II, whom he deposed, lost his.

KING HENRY

    . . . By being seldom seen, I could not stir
    But, like a comet, I was wondered at,
    That men would tell their children 'This is he.'
    Others would say 'Where, which is Bolingbroke?'
    And then I stole all courtesy from heaven,
    And dressed myself in such humility
    That I did pluck allegiance from men's hearts,
    Loud shouts and salutations from their mouths,
    Even in the presence of the crownèd King.
    Thus did I keep my person fresh and new,
    My presence like a robe pontifical—
    Ne'er seen but wondered at—and so my state,
    Seldom but sumptuous, showed like a feast,
    And won by rareness such solemnity.
    The skipping King, he ambled up and down
    With shallow jesters and rash bavin wits,
    Soon kindled and soon burnt, carded his state,
    Mingled his royalty with cap'ring fools,

Had his great name profanèd with their scorns,
And gave his countenance, against his name,
To laugh at gibing boys, and stand the push
Of every beardless vain comparative;
Grew a companion to the common streets,
Enfeoffed himself to popularity,
That, being daily swallowed by men's eyes,
They surfeited with honey, and began
To loathe the taste of sweetness, whereof a little
More than a little is by much too much.
So when he had occasion to be seen,
He was but as the cuckoo is in June,
Heard, not regarded, seen but with such eyes
As, sick and blunted with community,
Afford no extraordinary gaze
Such as is bent on sun-like majesty
When it shines seldom in admiring eyes,
But rather drowsed and hung their eyelids down,
Slept in his face, and rendered such aspect
As cloudy men use to their adversaries,
Being with his presence glutted, gorged, and full.

(*1 Henry IV*, 3.2.46–84)

A Queen's Defence

Henry VIII's first wife, Katherine (of Aragon), pleads against the King's desire to annul their marriage on the grounds that it is not valid.

SCRIBE (*to the Crier*)

> Say, 'Katherine, Queen of England, come into the court'.

CRIER

> Katherine, Queen of England, come into the court.
>> *The Queen makes no answer, but rises out of her chair, goes about the court, comes to King Henry VIII, and kneels at his feet. Then she speaks*

QUEEN KATHERINE

> Sir, I desire you do me right and justice,
> And to bestow your pity on me; for
> I am a most poor woman, and a stranger,
> Born out of your dominions, having here
> No judge indifferent, nor no more assurance
> Of equal friendship and proceeding. Alas, sir,
> In what have I offended you? What cause
> Hath my behaviour given to your displeasure
> That thus you should proceed to put me off,
> And take your good grace from me? Heaven witness
> I have been to you a true and humble wife,
> At all times to your will conformable,

Ever in fear to kindle your dislike,
Yea, subject to your countenance, glad or sorry
As I saw it inclined. When was the hour
I ever contradicted your desire,
Or made it not mine too? Or which of your friends
Have I not strove to love, although I knew
He were mine enemy? What friend of mine
That had to him derived your anger did I
Continue in my liking? Nay, gave notice
He was from thence discharged? Sir, call to mind
That I have been your wife in this obedience
Upward of twenty years, and have been blessed
With many children by you. If, in the course
And process of this time, you can report—
And prove it, too—against mine honour aught,
My bond to wedlock, or my love and duty
Against your sacred person, in God's name
Turn me away, and let the foul'st contempt
Shut door upon me, and so give me up
To the sharp'st kind of justice. Please you, sir,
The King your father was reputed for
A prince most prudent, of an excellent
And unmatched wit and judgement. Ferdinand
My father, King of Spain, was reckoned one
The wisest prince that there had reigned by many
A year before. It is not to be questioned
That they had gathered a wise council to them
Of every realm, that did debate this business,
Who deemed our marriage lawful. Wherefore I humbly

Beseech you, sir, to spare me till I may
Be by my friends in Spain advised, whose counsel
I will implore. If not, i'th' name of God,
Your pleasure be fulfilled.

(All is True (Henry VIII), 2.4.9–55)

Coriolanus (1)

At a meeting of the Senate, Cominius, Roman consul and commander-in-chief, speaks in praise of Coriolanus.

COMINIUS

I shall lack voice; the deeds of Coriolanus
Should not be uttered feebly. It is held
That valour is the chiefest virtue, and
Most dignifies the haver. If it be,
The man I speak of cannot in the world
Be singly counterpoised. At sixteen years,
When Tarquin made a head for Rome, he fought
Beyond the mark of others. Our then dictator,
Whom with all praise I point at, saw him fight
When with his Amazonian chin he drove
The bristled lips before him. He bestrid
An o'erpressed Roman, and, i'th' consul's view,
Slew three opposers. Tarquin's self he met,
And struck him on his knee. In that day's feats,
When he might act the woman in the scene,
He proved best man i'th' field, and for his meed
Was brow-bound with the oak. His pupil age
Man-entered thus, he waxèd like a sea,
And in the brunt of seventeen battles since
He lurched all swords of the garland. For this last
Before and in Corioles, let me say

I cannot speak him home. He stopped the fliers,
And by his rare example made the coward
Turn terror into sport. As weeds before
A vessel under sail, so men obeyed
And fell below his stem. His sword, death's stamp,
Where it did mark, it took. From face to foot
He was a thing of blood, whose every motion
Was timed with dying cries. Alone he entered
The mortal gate of th' city, which he, painted
With shunless destiny, aidless came off,
And with a sudden reinforcement struck
Corioles like a planet. Now all's his.
When by and by the din of war gan pierce
His ready sense, then straight his doubled spirit
Requickened what in flesh was fatigate,
And to the battle came he, where he did
Run reeking o'er the lives of men as if
'Twere a perpetual spoil; and till we called
Both field and city ours he never stood
To ease his breast with panting.

(*Coriolanus*, 2.2.82–122)

Coriolanus (2)

Coriolanus, exiled from Rome, now leads a Volscian army against his native city; the Volscian leader Aufidius plots against him.

AUFIDIUS

All places yields to him ere he sits down,
And the nobility of Rome are his.
The senators and patricians love him too.
The tribunes are no soldiers, and their people
Will be as rash in the repeal as hasty
To expel him thence. I think he'll be to Rome
As is the osprey to the fish, who takes it
By sovereignty of nature. First he was
A noble servant to them, but he could not
Carry his honours even. Whether 'twas pride,
Which out of daily fortune ever taints
The happy man; whether defect of judgement,
To fail in the disposing of those chances
Which he was lord of; or whether nature,
Not to be other than one thing, not moving
From th' casque to th' cushion, but commanding peace
Even with the same austerity and garb
As he controlled the war: but one of these—
As he hath spices of them all—not all,
For I dare so far free him—made him feared,
So hated, and so banished. But he has a merit

To choke it in the utt'rance. So our virtues
Lie in th'interpretation of the time,
And power, unto itself most commendable,
Hath not a tomb so evident as a chair
T'extol what it hath done.
One fire drives out one fire, one nail one nail;
Rights by rights falter, strengths by strengths do fail.
Come, let's away. When, Caius, Rome is thine,
Thou art poor'st of all; then shortly art thou mine.

(Coriolanus, 4.7.28–57)

Cassius

Julius Caesar speaks to Mark Antony about Cassius, not knowing that Cassius is planning his downfall.

CAESAR

    Let me have men about me that are fat,
    Sleek-headed men, and such as sleep a-nights.
    Yon Cassius has a lean and hungry look.
    He thinks too much. Such men are dangerous.

ANTONY

    Fear him not, Caesar, he's not dangerous.
    He is a noble Roman, and well given.

CAESAR

    Would he were fatter! But I fear him not.
    Yet if my name were liable to fear,
    I do not know the man I should avoid
    So soon as that spare Cassius. He reads much,
    He is a great observer, and he looks
    Quite through the deeds of men. He loves no plays,
    As thou dost, Antony; he hears no music.
    Seldom he smiles, and smiles in such a sort
    As if he mocked himself, and scorned his spirit
    That could be moved to smile at anything.
    Such men as he be never at heart's ease
    Whiles they behold a greater than themselves,
    And therefore are they very dangerous.

                     (Julius Caesar, 1.2.193–211)

Julius Caesar

Cassius speaks to his fellow-conspirator Brutus about Caesar.

CASSIUS
    . . . I was born free as Caesar, so were you.
    We both have fed as well, and we can both
    Endure the winter's cold as well as he.
    For once upon a raw and gusty day,
    The troubled Tiber chafing with her shores,
    Said Caesar to me 'Dar'st thou, Cassius, now
    Leap in with me into this angry flood,
    And swim to yonder point?' Upon the word,
    Accoutred as I was I plungèd in,
    And bade him follow. So indeed he did.
    The torrent roared, and we did buffet it
    With lusty sinews, throwing it aside,
    And stemming it with hearts of controversy.
    But ere we could arrive the point proposed,
    Caesar cried 'Help me, Cassius, or I sink!'
    Ay, as Aeneas our great ancestor
    Did from the flames of Troy upon his shoulder
    The old Anchises bear, so from the waves of Tiber
    Did I the tirèd Caesar. And this man
    Is now become a god, and Cassius is
    A wretched creature, and must bend his body
    If Caesar carelessly but nod on him.

He had a fever when he was in Spain,
And when the fit was on him, I did mark
How he did shake. 'Tis true, this god did shake.
His coward lips did from their colour fly;
And that same eye whose bend doth awe the world
Did lose his lustre. I did hear him groan,
Ay, and that tongue of his that bade the Romans
Mark him and write his speeches in their books,
'Alas!' it cried, 'Give me some drink, Titinius',
As a sick girl. Ye gods, it doth amaze me
A man of such a feeble temper should
So get the start of the majestic world,
And bear the palm alone!

(Julius Caesar, 1.2.99–133)

Mark Antony

After Mark Antony's death, Cleopatra speaks of him to Dolabella,
servant to her enemy Octavius Caesar.

CLEOPATRA

  I dreamt there was an Emperor Antony.
  O, such another sleep, that I might see
  But such another man!

DOLABELLA   If it might please ye—

CLEOPATRA

  His face was as the heav'ns, and therein stuck
  A sun and moon, which kept their course and lighted
  The little O o'th' earth.

DOLABELLA   Most sovereign creature—

CLEOPATRA

  His legs bestrid the ocean; his reared arm
  Crested the world. His voice was propertied
  As all the tunèd spheres, and that to friends;
  But when he meant to quail and shake the orb,
  He was as rattling thunder. For his bounty,
  There was no winter in't; an autumn 'twas,
  That grew the more by reaping. His delights
  Were dolphin-like; they showed his back above
  The element they lived in. In his livery
  Walked crowns and crownets. Realms and islands were
  As plates dropped from his pocket.

(Antony and Cleopatra, 5.2.75–91)

Cleopatra

Mark Antony's friend Enobarbus describes how Antony and he first saw Cleopatra.

ENOBARBUS

    . . . The barge she sat in, like a burnished throne
    Burned on the water. The poop was beaten gold;
    Purple the sails, and so perfumèd that
    The winds were love-sick with them. The oars were
      silver,
    Which to the tune of flutes kept stroke, and made
    The water which they beat to follow faster,
    As amorous of their strokes. For her own person,
    It beggared all description. She did lie
    In her pavilion—cloth of gold, of tissue—
    O'er-picturing that Venus where we see
    The fancy outwork nature. On each side her
    Stood pretty dimpled boys, like smiling Cupids,
    With divers-coloured fans whose wind did seem
    To glow the delicate cheeks which they did cool,
    And what they undid did.

AGRIPPA   O, rare for Antony!

ENOBARBUS

    Her gentlewomen, like the Nereides,
    So many mermaids, tended her i'th' eyes,
    And made their bends adornings. At the helm
    A seeming mermaid steers. The silken tackle

Swell with the touches of those flower-soft hands
That yarely frame the office. From the barge
A strange invisible perfume hits the sense
Of the adjacent wharfs. The city cast
Her people out upon her, and Antony,
Enthroned i'th' market-place, did sit alone,
Whistling to th'air, which but for vacancy
Had gone to gaze on Cleopatra too,
And made a gap in nature.

AGRIPPA   Rare Egyptian!

ENOBARBUS

Upon her landing Antony sent to her,
Invited her to supper. She replied
It should be better he became her guest,
Which she entreated. Our courteous Antony,
Whom ne'er the word of 'No' woman heard speak,
Being barbered ten times o'er, goes to the feast,
And for his ordinary pays his heart
For what his eyes eat only.

AGRIPPA   Royal wench!

She made great Caesar lay his sword to bed.
He ploughed her, and she cropped.

ENOBARBUS   I saw her once

Hop forty paces through the public street,
And having lost her breath, she spoke and panted,
That she did make defect perfection,
And breathless, pour breath forth.

MAECENAS   Now Antony

Must leave her utterly.

ENOBARBUS   Never. He will not.
  Age cannot wither her, nor custom stale
  Her infinite variety. Other women cloy
  The appetites they feed, but she makes hungry
  Where most she satisfies. For vilest things
  Become themselves in her, that the holy priests
  Bless her when she is riggish.
                    (*Antony and Cleopatra*, 2.2.198–246)

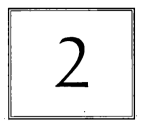

Friendship

'True love 'tween maid and maid'

Emilia, sister of Hippolyta (married to Theseus), tells of a childhood friendship.

EMILIA . . . I was acquainted
Once with a time when I enjoyed a playfellow,
You were at wars when she the grave enriched,
Who made too proud the bed; took leave o'th' moon—
Which then looked pale at parting—when our count
Was each eleven.
HIPPOLYTA 'Twas Flavina.
EMILIA Yes.
You talk of Pirithous' and Theseus' love:
Theirs has more ground, is more maturely seasoned,
More buckled with strong judgement, and their needs
The one of th'other may be said to water
Their intertangled roots of love; but I
And she I sigh and spoke of were things innocent,
Loved for we did, and like the elements,
That know not what, nor why, yet do effect
Rare issues by their operance, our souls
Did so to one another. What she liked
Was then of me approved; what not, condemned—
No more arraignment. The flower that I would pluck
And put between my breasts—O then but beginning
To swell about the blossom—she would long

Till she had such another, and commit it
To the like innocent cradle, where, phoenix-like,
They died in perfume. On my head no toy
But was her pattern. Her affections—pretty,
Though happily her careless wear—I followed
For my most serious decking. Had mine ear
Stol'n some new air, or at adventure hummed one,
From musical coinage, why, it was a note
Whereon her spirits would sojourn—rather dwell on—
And sing it in her slumbers. This rehearsal—
Which, seely innocence wots well, comes in
Like old emportment's bastard—has this end:
That the true love 'tween maid and maid may be
More than in sex dividual.

(*Two Noble Kinsmen*, 1.3.49–82)

A Boyhood Friendship

Hermione, Queen of Sicily, questions her husband's friend Polixenes
of their boyhood friendship.

HERMIONE   . . . Come, I'll question you
    Of my lord's tricks and yours when you were boys.
    You were pretty lordings then?
POLIXENES   We were, fair Queen,
    Two lads that thought there was no more behind
    But such a day tomorrow as today,
    And to be boy eternal.
HERMIONE Was not my lord
    The verier wag o'th' two?
POLIXENES
    We were as twinned lambs that did frisk i'th' sun,
    And bleat the one at th'other. What we changed
    Was innocence for innocence. We knew not
    The doctrine of ill-doing, nor dreamed
    That any did. Had we pursued that life,
    And our weak spirits ne'er been higher reared
    With stronger blood, we should have answered heaven
    Boldly, 'Not guilty', the imposition cleared
    Hereditary ours.
                   (The Winter's Tale, 1.2.61–77)

A Friend Forgiven

Full many a glorious morning have I seen
Flatter the mountain tops with sovereign eye,
Kissing with golden face the meadows green,
Gilding pale streams with heavenly alchemy;
Anon permit the basest clouds to ride
With ugly rack on his celestial face,
And from the forlorn world his visage hide,
Stealing unseen to west with this disgrace.
Even so my sun one early morn did shine
With all triumphant splendour on my brow;
But out, alack, he was but one hour mine;
The region cloud hath masked him from me now.
  Yet him for this my love no whit disdaineth:
  Suns of the world may stain when heaven's sun staineth.

(Sonnet 33)

Friendship Celebrated

When, in disgrace with fortune and men's eyes,
I all alone beweep my outcast state,
And trouble deaf heaven with my bootless cries,
And look upon myself and curse my fate,
Wishing me like to one more rich in hope,
Featured like him, like him with friends possessed,
Desiring this man's art and that man's scope,
With what I most enjoy contented least:
Yet in these thoughts myself almost despising,
Haply I think on thee, and then my state,
Like to the lark at break of day arising
From sullen earth, sings hymns at heaven's gate;
  For thy sweet love remembered such wealth brings
  That then I scorn to change my state with kings'.

(Sonnet 29)

True Friendship

Hamlet, Prince of Denmark, speaks with his fellow-student Horatio.

HAMLET

 Horatio, thou art e'en as just a man
 As e'er my conversation coped withal.

HORATIO

 O my dear lord—

HAMLET   Nay, do not think I flatter;
 For what advancement may I hope from thee,
 That no revenue hast but thy good spirits
 To feed and clothe thee? Why should the poor be
  flattered?
 No, let the candied tongue lick absurd pomp,
 And crook the pregnant hinges of the knee
 Where thrift may follow feigning. Dost thou hear?—
 Since my dear soul was mistress of her choice
 And could of men distinguish, her election
 Hath sealed thee for herself; for thou hast been
 As one in suff'ring all that suffers nothing,
 A man that Fortune's buffets and rewards
 Hath ta'en with equal thanks; and blest are those
 Whose blood and judgement are so well commingled
 That they are not a pipe for Fortune's finger
 To sound what stop she please. Give me that man
 That is not passion's slave, and I will wear him

In my heart's core, ay, in my heart of heart,
As I do thee.

(Hamlet, 3.2.52–72)

Man's Ingratitude

In the Forest of Ardenne Amiens sings to the exiled Duke and his companions.

AMIENS *(sings)*

>Blow, blow, thou winter wind,
>Thou art not so unkind
>>As man's ingratitude.
>Thy tooth is not so keen,
>Because thou art not seen,
>>Although thy breath be rude.
>Hey-ho, sing hey-ho, unto the green holly.
>Most friendship is feigning, most loving, mere folly.
>>Then hey-ho, the holly;
>>This life is most jolly.

>Freeze, freeze, thou bitter sky,
>That dost not bite so nigh
>>As benefits forgot.
>Though thou the waters warp,
>Thy sting is not so sharp
>>As friend remembered not.
>Hey-ho, sing hey-ho, unto the green holly.
>Most friendship is feigning, most loving, mere folly.
>>Then hey-ho, the holly;
>>This life is most jolly.

(As You Like It, 2.7.175–94)

Friendship Forsworn

Exiled from Rome, Coriolanus meditates before offering his services to his former enemy Aufidius at Antium.

CORIOLANUS

    . . . O world, thy slippery turns! Friends now fast
    sworn,
Whose double bosoms seem to wear one heart,
Whose hours, whose bed, whose meal and exercise
Are still together, who twin as 'twere in love
Unseparable, shall within this hour,
On a dissension of a doit, break out
To bitterest enmity. So fellest foes,
Whose passions and whose plots have broke their sleep
To take the one the other, by some chance,
Some trick not worth an egg, shall grow dear friends
And interjoin their issues. So with me.
My birthplace hate I, and my love's upon
This enemy town. I'll enter. If he slay me,
He does fair justice; if he give me way,
I'll do his country service.

                            (Coriolanus, 4.4.12–26)

Friendship and Love

Don Pedro, Prince of Aragon, has been wooing Hero on Claudio's behalf; now Claudio is led to suspect that 'the Prince woos for himself'.

CLAUDIO

     . . . Friendship is constant in all other things
     Save in the office and affairs of love.
     Therefore all hearts in love use their own tongues.
     Let every eye negotiate for itself,
     And trust no agent; for beauty is a witch
     Against whose charms faith melteth into blood.

                (*Much Ado About Nothing*, 2.1.165–70)

Father and Son

Leontes, King of Sicily, suspects that Polixenes, King of Bohemia, has cuckolded him; looking at his son Mamillius, Leontes recalls his own boyhood.

LEONTES
... How sometimes nature will betray its folly,
Its tenderness, and make itself a pastime
To harder bosoms! Looking on the lines
Of my boy's face, methoughts I did recoil
Twenty-three years, and saw myself unbreeched,
In my green velvet coat; my dagger muzzled,
Lest it should bite its master, and so prove,
As ornament oft does, too dangerous.
How like, methought, I then was to this kernel,
This squash, this gentleman.—Mine honest friend,
Will you take eggs for money?

MAMILLIUS   No, my lord, I'll fight.

LEONTES
You will? Why, happy man be's dole!—My brother,
Are you so fond of your young prince as we
Do seem to be of ours?

POLIXENES   If at home, sir,
He's all my exercise, my mirth, my matter;
Now my sworn friend, and then mine enemy;
My parasite, my soldier, statesman, all.

He makes a July's day short as December,
And with his varying childness cures in me
Thoughts that would thick my blood.

LEONTES   So stands this squire
Officed with me.

(The Winter's Tale, 1.2.153–73)

A Man and his Dog

Proteus has sent his servant Lance to present a dog to his beloved, Silvia.

Enter Lance and his dog Crab

LANCE (*to the audience*) When a man's servant shall play the cur with him, look you, it goes hard. One that I brought up of a puppy, one that I saved from drowning when three or four of his blind brothers and sisters went to it. I have taught him, even as one would say precisely 'Thus I would teach a dog'. I was sent to deliver him as a present to Mistress Silvia from my master, and I came no sooner into the dining-chamber but he steps me to her trencher and steals her capon's leg. O, 'tis a foul thing when a cur cannot keep himself in all companies. I would have, as one should say, one that takes upon him to be a dog indeed, to be, as it were, a dog at all things. If I had not had more wit than he, to take a fault upon me that he did, I think verily he had been hanged for't. Sure as I live, he had suffered for't. You shall judge. He thrusts me himself into the company of three or four gentleman-like dogs under the Duke's table. He had not been there—bless the mark—a pissing-while but all the chamber smelled him. 'Out with the dog,' says one. 'What cur is that?' says another. 'Whip him out,' says the third. 'Hang him up,' says the Duke. I, having been acquainted with the smell before, knew it was Crab, and goes me to the fellow that whips the dogs. 'Friend,' quoth I, 'you mean to whip the dog.' 'Ay, marry do I,' quoth he. 'You do him the more wrong,' quoth I, ''twas I did the thing you wot of.' He makes me no more ado, but whips me out of the chamber. How many masters would do this for his servant? Nay, I'll be sworn I have sat in the stocks for puddings he hath stolen, otherwise he had been executed. I have stood on the pillory for geese he hath killed, otherwise he had suffered for't. (*To Crab*) Thou think'st not of this now. Nay, I remember the trick you served me when I took my leave of Madam Silvia. Did not I bid thee still mark me, and do as I do? When didst thou see me heave up my leg and make water against a gentlewoman's farthingale? Didst thou ever see me do such a trick?

(*The Two Gentlemen of Verona*, 4.4.1–38)

Love

First Love

Montague and his wife speak with their nephew Benvolio of their son
Romeo's love for Rosaline.

MONTAGUE'S WIFE

    O where is Romeo—saw you him today?

    Right glad I am he was not at this fray.

BENVOLIO

    Madam, an hour before the worshipped sun

    Peered forth the golden window of the east,

    A troubled mind drive me to walk abroad,

    Where, underneath the grove of sycamore

    That westward rooteth from this city side,

    So early walking did I see your son.

    Towards him I made, but he was ware of me,

    And stole into the covert of the wood.

    I, measuring his affections by my own—

    Which then most sought where most might not be
       found,

    Being one too many by my weary self—

    Pursued my humour not pursuing his,

    And gladly shunned who gladly fled from me.

MONTAGUE

    Many a morning hath he there been seen,

    With tears augmenting the fresh morning's dew,

    Adding to clouds more clouds with his deep sighs.

But all so soon as the all-cheering sun
Should in the farthest east begin to draw
The shady curtains from Aurora's bed,
Away from light steals home my heavy son,
And private in his chamber pens himself,
Shuts up his windows, locks fair daylight out,
And makes himself an artificial night.
Black and portentous must this humour prove,
Unless good counsel may the cause remove.

BENVOLIO

My noble uncle, do you know the cause?

MONTAGUE

I neither know it nor can learn of him.

BENVOLIO

Have you importuned him by any means?

MONTAGUE

Both by myself and many other friends,
But he, his own affection's counsellor,
Is to himself—I will not say how true,
But to himself so secret and so close,
So far from sounding and discovery,
As is the bud bit with an envious worm
Ere he can spread his sweet leaves to the air
Or dedicate his beauty to the sun.
Could we but learn from whence his sorrows grow
We would as willingly give cure as know.

(Romeo and Juliet, 1.1.113–52)

How to Know a Man in Love

Valentine's servant Speed has observed his master's love for Silvia.

VALENTINE . . . Tell me, do you know Madam Silvia?
SPEED She that your worship loves?
VALENTINE Why, how know you that I am in love?
SPEED Marry, by these special marks: first, you have learned,
     like Sir Proteus, to wreath your arms, like a malcontent; to
     relish a love-song, like a robin redbreast; to walk alone, like
     one that had the pestilence; to sigh, like a schoolboy that
     had lost his ABC; to weep, like a young wench that had
     buried her grandam; to fast, like one that takes diet; to
     watch, like one that fears robbing; to speak puling, like a
     beggar at Hallowmas. You were wont, when you laughed,
     to crow like a cock; when you walked, to walk like one of the
     lions. When you fasted, it was presently after dinner; when
     you looked sadly, it was for want of money. And now you
     are metamorphosed with a mistress, that when I look on
     you I can hardly think you my master.

(*The Two Gentlemen of Verona*, 2.1.13–30)

A Cure for Love

Orlando, in love with Rosalind, does not know her in her disguise as Ganymede.

ROSALIND ... There is a man haunts the forest that abuses our young plants with carving Rosalind on their barks; hangs odes upon hawthorns and elegies on brambles; all, forsooth, deifying the name of Rosalind. If I could meet that fancy-monger, I would give him some good counsel, for he seems to have the quotidian of love upon him.

ORLANDO I am he that is so love-shaked. I pray you, tell me your remedy.

ROSALIND There is none of my uncle's marks upon you. He taught me how to know a man in love, in which cage of rushes I am sure you are not prisoner.

ORLANDO What were his marks?

ROSALIND A lean cheek, which you have not; a blue eye and sunken, which you have not; an unquestionable spirit, which you have not; a beard neglected, which you have not—but I pardon you for that, for simply your having in beard is a younger brother's revenue. Then your hose should be ungartered, your bonnet unbanded, your sleeve unbuttoned, your shoe untied, and everything about you demonstrating a careless desolation. But you are no such man. You are rather point-device in your accoutrements, as loving yourself than seeming the lover of any other.

ORLANDO Fair youth, I would I could make thee believe I love.

ROSALIND Me believe it? You may as soon make her that you love believe it, which I warrant she is apter to do than to confess she does. That is one of the points in the which women still give the lie to their consciences. But in good sooth, are you he that hangs the verses on the trees wherein Rosalind is so admired?

ORLANDO I swear to thee, youth, by the white hand of Rosalind, I am that he, that unfortunate he.

ROSALIND But are you so much in love as your rhymes speak?

ORLANDO Neither rhyme nor reason can express how much.

ROSALIND Love is merely a madness, and I tell you, deserves as well a dark house and a whip as madmen do; and the reason why they are not so punished and cured is that the lunacy is so ordinary that the whippers are in love too. Yet I profess curing it by counsel.

ORLANDO Did you ever cure any so?

ROSALIND Yes, one; and in this manner. He was to imagine me his love, his mistress; and I set him every day to woo me. At which time would I, being but a moonish youth, grieve, be effeminate, changeable, longing and liking, proud, fantastical, apish, shallow, inconstant, full of tears, full of smiles; for every passion something, and for no passion truly anything, as boys and women are for the most part cattle of this colour—would now like him, now loathe him; then entertain him, then forswear him; now weep for him, then spit at him, that I drave my suitor from his mad humour of love to a living humour of madness, which was to forswear the full stream of the world and to live in a nook merely

monastic. And thus I cured him, and this way will I take
upon me to wash your liver as clean as a sound sheep's
heart, that there shall not be one spot of love in't.

ORLANDO I would not be cured, youth.

ROSALIND I would cure you if you would but call me Rosalind
and come every day to my cot, and woo me.

ORLANDO Now by the faith of my love, I will. Tell me where it
is.

ROSALIND Go with me to it, and I'll show it you. And by the
way you shall tell me where in the forest you live. Will you
go?

ORLANDO With all my heart, good youth.

ROSALIND Nay, you must call me Rosalind.—Come, sister.
Will you go?   *Exeunt*

A Lover's Folly Described

*Benedick, the confirmed bachelor, contemplates his friend Claudio's
descent into a lover.*

BENEDICK . . . I do much wonder that one man, seeing how
much another man is a fool when he dedicates his
behaviours to love, will, after he hath laughed at such
shallow follies in others, become the argument of his own
scorn by falling in love. And such a man is Claudio. I have
known when there was no music with him but the drum and
the fife, and now had he rather hear the tabor and the pipe. I
have known when he would have walked ten mile afoot to
see a good armour, and now will he lie ten nights awake
carving the fashion of a new doublet. He was wont to speak
plain and to the purpose, like an honest man and a soldier,
and now is he turned orthography. His words are a very
fantastical banquet, just so many strange dishes. May I be
so converted, and see with these eyes? I cannot tell. I think
not. I will not be sworn but love may transform me to an
oyster, but I'll take my oath on it, till he have made an
oyster of me he shall never make me such a fool. One
woman is fair, yet I am well. Another is wise, yet I am well.
Another virtuous, yet I am well. But till all graces be in one
woman, one woman shall not come in my grace. Rich she
shall be, that's certain. Wise, or I'll none. Virtuous, or I'll
never cheapen her. Fair, or I'll never look on her. Mild, or

come not near me. Noble, or not I for an angel. Of good discourse, an excellent musician, and her hair shall be of what colour it please God.

(Much Ado About Nothing, 2.3.8–34)

A Misogynist in Love

Biron contemplates his own capitulation to love.

BIRON

And I, forsooth, in love—I that have been love's whip,
A very beadle to a humorous sigh,
A critic, nay, a night-watch constable,
A domineering pedant o'er the boy,
Than whom no mortal so magnificent.
This wimpled, whining, purblind, wayward boy,
This Signor Junior, giant dwarf, Dan Cupid,
Regent of love-rhymes, lord of folded arms,
Th'anointed sovereign of sighs and groans,
Liege of all loiterers and malcontents,
Dread prince of plackets, king of codpieces,
Sole imperator and great general
Of trotting paritors—O my little heart!
And I to be a corporal of his field,
And wear his colours like a tumbler's hoop!
What? I love, I sue, I seek a wife?—
A woman, that is like a German clock,
Still a-repairing, ever out of frame,
And never going aright, being a watch,
But being watched that it may still go right.
Nay, to be perjured, which is worst of all,
And among three to love the worst of all—

A whitely wanton with a velvet brow,
With two pitch-balls stuck in her face for eyes—
Ay, and, by heaven, one that will do the deed
Though Argus were her eunuch and her guard.
And I to sigh for her, to watch for her,
To pray for her—go to, it is a plague
That Cupid will impose for my neglect
Of his almighty dreadful little might.
Well, I will love, write, sigh, pray, sue, groan:
Some men must love my lady, and some Joan.

(*Love's Labour's Lost*, 3.1.169–200)

A First Kiss

At a party, Romeo speaks for the first time to Juliet, daughter of his family's long-standing enemies.

ROMEO *(to Juliet, touching her hand)*
>If I profane with my unworthiest hand
>>This holy shrine, the gentler sin is this:
>My lips, two blushing pilgrims, ready stand
>>To smooth that rough touch with a tender kiss.

JULIET
>Good pilgrim, you do wrong your hand too much,
>>Which mannerly devotion shows in this.
>For saints have hands that pilgrims' hands do touch,
>>And palm to palm is holy palmers' kiss.

ROMEO
>Have not saints lips, and holy palmers, too?

JULIET
>Ay, pilgrim, lips that they must use in prayer.

ROMEO
>O then, dear saint, let lips do what hands do:
>>They pray; grant thou, lest faith turn to despair.

JULIET
>Saints do not move, though grant for prayers' sake.

ROMEO
>Then move not while my prayer's effect I take.
>>*He kisses her*

Thus from my lips, by thine my sin is purged.

JULIET

Then have my lips the sin that they have took.

ROMEO

Sin from my lips? O trespass sweetly urged!
Give me my sin again.

He kisses her

JULIET   You kiss by th' book.

(Romeo and Juliet, 1.5.92–109)

Love Concealed

Disguised as a boy, Cesario, Viola speaks to the Duke, Orsino, whom she loves.

VIOLA
   . . . My father had a daughter loved a man
   As it might be, perhaps, were I a woman
   I should your lordship.
ORSINO   And what's her history?
VIOLA
   A blank, my lord. She never told her love,
   But let concealment, like a worm i'th' bud,
   Feed on her damask cheek. She pined in thought,
   And with a green and yellow melancholy
   She sat like patience on a monument,
   Smiling at grief. Was not this love indeed?
   We men may say more, swear more, but indeed
   Our shows are more than will; for still we prove
   Much in our vows, but little in our love.
ORSINO
   But died thy sister of her love, my boy?
VIOLA
   I am all the daughters of my father's house,
   And all the brothers too; and yet I know not.
                    (Twelfth Night, 2.4.107–21)

Song of an Unrequited Lover

The lovesick Duke Orsino tells the fool, Feste, to sing to him and to Cesario (actually Viola, secretly in love with Orsino).

ORSINO *(to Feste)*
O fellow, come, the song we had last night.
Mark it, Cesario, it is old and plain.
The spinsters, and the knitters in the sun,
And the free maids that weave their thread with bones,
Do use to chant it. It is silly sooth,
And dallies with the innocence of love,
Like the old age.
FESTE Are you ready, sir?
ORSINO I prithee, sing.
    Music

FESTE *(sings)*
Come away, come away death,
  And in sad cypress let me be laid.
Fie away, fie away breath,
  I am slain by a fair cruel maid.
My shroud of white, stuck all with yew,
    O prepare it.
My part of death no one so true
    Did share it.

Not a flower, not a flower sweet
  On my black coffin let there be strewn.
Not a friend, not a friend greet
  My poor corpse, where my bones shall be thrown.
A thousand thousand sighs to save,
    Lay me O where
Sad true lover never find my grave,
    To weep there.

(Twelfth Night, 2.4.41–65)

A Fearful Love

The humble Helen speaks of her unacknowledged love for Bertram, Count of Roussillon, who is leaving the home where they have grown up together.

HELEN   . . . My imagination
    Carries no favour in't but Bertram's.
    I am undone. There is no living, none,
    If Bertram be away. 'Twere all one
    That I should love a bright particular star
    And think to wed it, he is so above me.
    In his bright radiance and collateral light
    Must I be comforted, not in his sphere.
    Th'ambition in my love thus plagues itself.
    The hind that would be mated by the lion
    Must die for love. 'Twas pretty, though a plague,
    To see him every hour, to sit and draw
    His archèd brows, his hawking eye, his curls,
    In our heart's table—heart too capable
    Of every line and trick of his sweet favour.
    But now he's gone, and my idolatrous fancy
    Must sanctify his relics.
                      (All's Well That Ends Well, 1.1.81–97)

Unwanted Love

Helen's husband, the Count of Roussillon, has gone to the wars rather than consummate their marriage.

HELEN   . . . Poor lord, is't I
    That chase thee from thy country and expose
    Those tender limbs of thine to the event
    Of the none-sparing war? And is it I
    That drive thee from the sportive court, where thou
    Wast shot at with fair eyes, to be the mark
    Of smoky muskets? O you leaden messengers
    That ride upon the violent speed of fire,
    Fly with false aim, cleave the still-piecing air
    That sings with piercing, do not touch my lord.
    Whoever shoots at him, I set him there.
    Whoever charges on his forward breast,
    I am the caitiff that do hold him to't,
    And though I kill him not, I am the cause
    His death was so effected. Better 'twere
    I met the ravin lion when he roared
    With sharp constraint of hunger; better 'twere
    That all the miseries which nature owes
    Were mine at once. No, come thou home, Roussillon,
    Whence honour but of danger wins a scar,
    As oft it loses all. I will be gone;
    My being here it is that holds thee hence.

Shall I stay here to do't? No, no, although
The air of paradise did fan the house
And angels officed all. I will be gone,
That pitiful rumour may report my flight
To consolate thine ear. Come night, end day;
For with the dark, poor thief, I'll steal away.   *Exit*

(*All's Well That Ends Well*, 3.2.104–31)

A Jester's Courtship

The clown and jester Touchstone admits to his mistress Rosalind that he was once in love.

TOUCHSTONE ... I remember when I was in love I broke my
sword upon a stone and bid him take that for coming a-night
to Jane Smile, and I remember the kissing of her batlet, and
the cow's dugs that her pretty chapped hands had milked;
and I remember the wooing of a peascod instead of her, from
whom I took two cods, and giving her them again, said with
weeping tears, 'Wear these for my sake.' We that are true
lovers run into strange capers. But as all is mortal in nature,
so is all nature in love mortal in folly.
ROSALIND Thou speak'st wiser than thou art ware of.
TOUCHSTONE Nay, I shall ne'er be ware of mine own wit till I
break my shins against it.

(As You Like It, 2.4.43–55)

A Lesson in Wooing

Proteus, while wooing Silvia for himself, advises his rival Thurio how to woo her.

PROTEUS

> Say that upon the altar of her beauty
> You sacrifice your tears, your sighs, your heart.
> Write till your ink be dry, and with your tears
> Moist it again; and frame some feeling line
> That may discover such integrity;
> For Orpheus' lute was strung with poets' sinews,
> Whose golden touch could soften steel and stones,
> Make tigers tame, and huge leviathans
> Forsake unsounded deeps to dance on sands.
> After your dire-lamenting elegies,
> Visit by night your lady's chamber-window
> With some sweet consort. To their instruments
> Tune a deploring dump. The night's dead silence
> Will well become such sweet-complaining grievance.
> This, or else nothing, will inherit her.
>
> *(The Two Gentlemen of Verona, 3.2.72–86)*

The Spirit of Love

The lovesick Duke Orsino feeds his passion with music.

ORSINO

If music be the food of love, play on,
Give me excess of it that, surfeiting,
The appetite may sicken and so die.
That strain again, it had a dying fall.
O, it came o'er my ear like the sweet sound
That breathes upon a bank of violets,
Stealing and giving odour. Enough, no more,
'Tis not so sweet now as it was before.
    Music ceases
O spirit of love, how quick and fresh art thou
That, notwithstanding thy capacity
Receiveth as the sea, naught enters there,
Of what validity and pitch so e'er,
But falls into abatement and low price
Even in a minute! So full of shapes is fancy
That it alone is high fantastical.
                (Twelfth Night, 1.1.1–15)

A Banished Lover

The Duke of Milan, having unmasked Valentine's plot to elope with his daughter Silvia, has banished him.

DUKE

   . . . Be gone. I will not hear thy vain excuse,
   But as thou lov'st thy life, make speed from hence. *Exit*

VALENTINE

   And why not death, rather than living torment?
   To die is to be banished from myself,
   And Silvia is my self. Banished from her
   Is self from self, a deadly banishment.
   What light is light, if Silvia be not seen?
   What joy is joy, if Silvia be not by—
   Unless it be to think that she is by,
   And feed upon the shadow of perfection.
   Except I be by Silvia in the night
   There is no music in the nightingale.
   Unless I look on Silvia in the day
   There is no day for me to look upon.
   She is my essence, and I leave to be
   If I be not by her fair influence
   Fostered, illumined, cherished, kept alive.
   I fly not death to fly his deadly doom.
   Tarry I here I but attend on death,
   But fly I hence, I fly away from life.

               (*The Two Gentlemen of Verona*, 3.1.168–87)

A Vow Renounced

Biron demonstrates that he and his friends are right to renounce their vows not to fall in love.

BIRON

... Consider what you first did swear unto:
To fast, to study, and to see no woman—
Flat treason 'gainst the kingly state of youth.
Say, can you fast? Your stomachs are too young,
And abstinence engenders maladies.
O, we have made a vow to study, lords,
And in that vow we have forsworn our books;
For when would you, my liege, or you, or you
In leaden contemplation have found out
Such fiery numbers as the prompting eyes
Of beauty's tutors have enriched you with?
Other slow arts entirely keep the brain,
And therefore, finding barren practisers,
Scarce show a harvest of their heavy toil.
But love, first learnèd in a lady's eyes,
Lives not alone immurèd in the brain,
But with the motion of all elements
Courses as swift as thought in every power,
And gives to every power a double power
Above their functions and their offices.
It adds a precious seeing to the eye—

A lover's eyes will gaze an eagle blind.
A lover's ear will hear the lowest sound
When the suspicious head of theft is stopped.
Love's feeling is more soft and sensible
Than are the tender horns of cockled snails.
Love's tongue proves dainty Bacchus gross in taste.
For valour, is not love a Hercules,
Still climbing trees in the Hesperides?
Subtle as Sphinx, as sweet and musical
As bright Apollo's lute strung with his hair;
And when love speaks, the voice of all the gods
Make heaven drowsy with the harmony.
Never durst poet touch a pen to write
Until his ink were tempered with love's sighs.
O, then his lines would ravish savage ears,
And plant in tyrants mild humility.
From women's eyes this doctrine I derive.
They sparkle still the right Promethean fire.
They are the books, the arts, the academes
That show, contain, and nourish all the world,
Else none at all in aught proves excellent.
Then fools you were these women to forswear,
Or keeping what is sworn, you will prove fools.
For wisdom's sake—a word that all men love—
Or for love's sake—a word that loves all men—
Or for men's sake—the authors of these women—
Or women's sake—by whom we men are men—
Let us once lose our oaths to find ourselves,
Or else we lose ourselves to keep our oaths.

It is religion to be thus forsworn,
For charity itself fulfils the law,
And who can sever love from charity?
　　　　(*Love's Labour's Lost*, 4.3.289–341)

A Declaration

After the party at the Capulets' house at which Romeo has fallen in love with Juliet, he is left alone in the garden.

ROMEO *(coming forward)*

 . . . But soft, what light through yonder window
   breaks?
It is the east, and Juliet is the sun.
Arise, fair sun, and kill the envious moon,
Who is already sick and pale with grief
That thou, her maid, art far more fair than she.
Be not her maid, since she is envious.
Her vestal livery is but sick and green,
And none but fools do wear it; cast it off.
   Enter Juliet aloft
It is my lady, O, it is my love.
O that she knew she were!
She speaks, yet she says nothing. What of that?
Her eye discourses; I will answer it.
I am too bold. 'Tis not to me she speaks.
Two of the fairest stars in all the heaven,
Having some business, do entreat her eyes
To twinkle in their spheres till they return.
What if her eyes were there, they in her head?—
The brightness of her cheek would shame those stars
As daylight doth a lamp; her eye in heaven

Would through the airy region stream so bright
That birds would sing and think it were not night.
See how she leans her cheek upon her hand.
O, that I were a glove upon that hand,
That I might touch that cheek!

JULIET   Ay me.

ROMEO (*aside*)   She speaks.

O, speak again, bright angel; for thou art
As glorious to this night, being o'er my head,
As is a wingèd messenger of heaven
Unto the white upturnèd wond'ring eyes
Of mortals that fall back to gaze on him
When he bestrides the lazy-passing clouds
And sails upon the bosom of the air.

JULIET (*not knowing Romeo hears her*)

O Romeo, Romeo, wherefore art thou Romeo?
Deny thy father and refuse thy name,
Or if thou wilt not, be but sworn my love,
And I'll no longer be a Capulet.

ROMEO (*aside*)

Shall I hear more, or shall I speak at this?

JULIET

'Tis but thy name that is my enemy.
Thou art thyself, though not a Montague.
What's Montague? It is nor hand, nor foot,
Nor arm, nor face, nor any other part
Belonging to a man. O, be some other name!
What's in a name? That which we call a rose
By any other word would smell as sweet.

So Romeo would, were he not Romeo called,
Retain that dear perfection which he owes
Without that title. Romeo, doff thy name,
And for thy name—which is no part of thee—
Take all myself.

ROMEO (*to Juliet*)   I take thee at thy word.
Call me but love and I'll be new baptized.
Henceforth I never will be Romeo.

(*Romeo and Juliet*, 2.1.44–93)

Love's Lottery

*Portia speaks as Bassanio, whom she loves, makes the choice that will
determine whether he wins her hand in marriage.*

PORTIA
> . . . Let music sound while he doth make his choice.
> Then if he lose he makes a swanlike end,
> Fading in music. That the comparison
> May stand more proper, my eye shall be the stream
> And wat'ry deathbed for him. He may win,
> And what is music then? Then music is
> Even as the flourish when true subjects bow
> To a new-crownèd monarch. Such it is
> As are those dulcet sounds in break of day
> That creep into the dreaming bridegroom's ear
> And summon him to marriage. Now he goes,
> With no less presence but with much more love
> Than young Alcides when he did redeem
> The virgin tribute paid by howling Troy
> To the sea-monster. I stand for sacrifice.
> The rest aloof are the Dardanian wives,
> With blearèd visages come forth to view
> The issue of th'exploit. Go, Hercules.
> Live thou, I live. With much much more dismay
> I view the fight than thou that mak'st the fray.

(The Merchant of Venice, 3.2.43–62)

Love Celebrated

Shall I compare thee to a summer's day?
Thou art more lovely and more temperate.
Rough winds do shake the darling buds of May,
And summer's lease hath all too short a date.
Sometime too hot the eye of heaven shines,
And often is his gold complexion dimmed,
And every fair from fair sometime declines,
By chance or nature's changing course untrimmed;
But thy eternal summer shall not fade
Nor lose possession of that fair thou ow'st,
Nor shall death brag thou wander'st in his shade
When in eternal lines to time thou grow'st.
  So long as men can breathe or eyes can see,
  So long lives this, and this gives life to thee.

(Sonnet 18)

The Course of True Love

Theseus, Duke of Athens, has supported Egeus in opposing the marriage of Egeus' daughter Hermia to Lysander, whom she loves.

LYSANDER

How now, my love? Why is your cheek so pale?
How chance the roses there do fade so fast?

HERMIA

Belike for want of rain, which I could well
Beteem them from the tempest of my eyes.

LYSANDER

Ay me, for aught that I could ever read,
Could ever hear by tale or history,
The course of true love never did run smooth,
But either it was different in blood—

HERMIA

O cross!—too high to be enthralled to low.

LYSANDER

Or else misgrafted in respect of years—

HERMIA

O spite!—too old to be engaged to young.

LYSANDER

Or merit stood upon the choice of friends—

HERMIA

O hell!—to choose love by another's eyes.

LYSANDER

Or if there were a sympathy in choice,

War, death, or sickness did lay siege to it,
Making it momentany as a sound,
Swift as a shadow, short as any dream,
Brief as the lightning in the collied night,
That, in a spleen, unfolds both heaven and earth,
And, ere a man hath power to say 'Behold!',
The jaws of darkness do devour it up.
So quick bright things come to confusion.

(*A Midsummer Night's Dream*, 1.1.128–49)

A Love Scene

Miranda has been brought up since infancy by her father Prospero, the exiled Duke of Milan, on a desert island; now Prospero, exercising his magical powers through his agent Ariel, causes her to see a young man—Ferdinand, Prince of Naples—for the first time.

PROSPERO *(to Miranda)*
    The fringèd curtains of thine eye advance,
    And say what thou seest yon.
MIRANDA   What is't? A spirit?
    Lord, how it looks about! Believe me, sir,
    It carries a brave form. But 'tis a spirit.
PROSPERO
    No, wench, it eats and sleeps, and hath such senses
    As we have, such. This gallant which thou seest
    Was in the wreck, and but he's something stained
    With grief, that's beauty's canker, thou mightst call him
    A goodly person. He hath lost his fellows,
    And strays about to find 'em.
MIRANDA   I might call him
    A thing divine, for nothing natural
    I ever saw so noble.
PROSPERO *(aside)*   It goes on, I see,
    As my soul prompts it. *(To Ariel)* Spirit, fine spirit, I'll
      free thee
    Within two days for this.

FERDINAND (*aside*)   Most sure the goddess
 On whom these airs attend. (*To Miranda*) Vouchsafe my
  prayer
 May know if you remain upon this island,
 And that you will some good instruction give
 How I may bear me here. My prime request,
 Which I do last pronounce, is—O you wonder—
 If you be maid or no?

MIRANDA   No wonder, sir,
 But certainly a maid.

FERDINAND   My language! Heavens!
 I am the best of them that speak this speech,
 Were I but where 'tis spoken.

PROSPERO   How, the best?
 What wert thou if the King of Naples heard thee?

FERDINAND
 A single thing, as I am now that wonders
 To hear thee speak of Naples. He does hear me,
 And that he does I weep. Myself am Naples,
 Who with mine eyes, never since at ebb, beheld
 The King my father wrecked.

MIRANDA   Alack, for mercy!

FERDINAND
 Yes, faith, and all his lords, the Duke of Milan
 And his brave son being twain.

PROSPERO (*aside*)   The Duke of Milan
 And his more braver daughter could control thee,
 If now 'twere fit to do't. At the first sight
 They have changed eyes.—Delicate Ariel,

I'll set thee free for this. (*To Ferdinand*) A word, good
    sir.
I fear you have done yourself some wrong. A word.

MIRANDA (*aside*)
    Why speaks my father so ungently? This
    Is the third man that e'er I saw, the first
    That e'er I sighed for. Pity move my father
    To be inclined my way.

FERDINAND   O, if a virgin,
    And your affection not gone forth, I'll make you
    The Queen of Naples.

PROSPERO   Soft, sir! One word more.
    (*Aside*) They are both in either's powers. But this swift
      business
    I must uneasy make, lest too light winning
    Make the prize light. (*To Ferdinand*) One word more. I
      charge thee
    That thou attend me. Thou dost here usurp
    The name thou ow'st not; and hast put thyself
    Upon this island as a spy, to win it
    From me the lord on't.

FERDINAND   No, as I am a man.

MIRANDA
    There's nothing ill can dwell in such a temple.
    If the ill spirit have so fair a house,
    Good things will strive to dwell with't.

PROSPERO (*to Ferdinand*)   Follow me.
    (*To Miranda*) Speak not you for him; he's a traitor. (*To
    Ferdinand*) Come!

I'll manacle thy neck and feet together.
Sea-water shalt thou drink; thy food shall be
The fresh-brook mussels, withered roots, and husks
Wherein the acorn cradled. Follow!

FERDINAND   No.
I will resist such entertainment till
Mine enemy has more power.

He draws, and is charmed from moving

MIRANDA   O dear father,
Make not too rash a trial of him, for
He's gentle, and not fearful.

PROSPERO   What, I say,
My foot my tutor? Put thy sword up, traitor,
Who mak'st a show but dar'st not strike, thy conscience
Is so possessed with guilt. Come from thy ward,
For I can here disarm thee with this stick
And make thy weapon drop.

MIRANDA   Beseech you, father!

PROSPERO
Hence! Hang not on my garments.

MIRANDA   Sir, have pity.
I'll be his surety.

PROSPERO   Silence! One word more
Shall make me chide thee, if not hate thee. What,
An advocate for an impostor? Hush!
Thou think'st there is no more such shapes as he,
Having seen but him and Caliban. Foolish wench!
To th' most of men this is a Caliban,
And they to him are angels.

MIRANDA   My affections
    Are then most humble. I have no ambition
    To see a goodlier man.
PROSPERO *(to Ferdinand)*   Come on; obey.
    Thy nerves are in their infancy again,
    And have no vigour in them.
FERDINAND   So they are.
    My spirits, as in a dream, are all bound up.
    My father's loss, the weakness which I feel,
    The wreck of all my friends, nor this man's threats
    To whom I am subdued, are but light to me,
    Might I but through my prison once a day
    Behold this maid. All corners else o'th' earth
    Let liberty make use of; space enough
    Have I in such a prison.
PROSPERO *(aside)*   It works. *(To Ferdinand)* Come on.—
    Thou hast done well, fine Ariel. *(To Ferdinand)* Follow me.
    (To Ariel) Hark what thou else shalt do me.
MIRANDA *(to Ferdinand)*   Be of comfort.
    My father's of a better nature, sir,
    Than he appears by speech. This is unwonted
    Which now came from him.
PROSPERO *(to Ariel)*   Thou shalt be as free
    As mountain winds; but then exactly do
    All points of my command.
ARIEL To th' syllable.
PROSPERO *(to Ferdinand)*
    Come, follow. *(To Miranda)* Speak not for him.   *Exeunt*
                               (The Tempest, 1.2.412–506)

Love's Blossoming

*Perdita, daughter of Leontes, King of Sicily, but brought up as a
Bohemian shepherdess, speaks at a sheep-shearing feast to her lover
Florizel, the disguised Prince of Bohemia.*

PERDITA . . . (*To Florizel*)   Now, my fair'st friend,
  I would I had some flowers o'th' spring that might
  Become your time of day; (*to Mopsa and Dorcas*) and
      yours, and yours,
  That wear upon your virgin branches yet
  Your maidenheads growing. O Proserpina,
  For the flowers now that, frighted, thou letst fall
  From Dis's wagon!—daffodils,
  That come before the swallow dares, and take
  The winds of March with beauty; violets, dim,
  But sweeter than the lids of Juno's eyes
  Or Cytherea's breath; pale primroses,
  That die unmarried ere they can behold
  Bright Phoebus in his strength—a malady
  Most incident to maids; bold oxlips, and
  The crown imperial; lilies of all kinds,
  The flower-de-luce being one. O, these I lack,
  To make you garlands of, and my sweet friend,
  To strew him o'er and o'er.
FLORIZEL   What, like a corpse?

PERDITA

No, like a bank, for love to lie and play on,
Not like a corpse—or if, not to be buried,
But quick and in mine arms. Come, take your flowers.
Methinks I play as I have seen them do
In Whitsun pastorals. Sure this robe of mine
Does change my disposition.

FLORIZEL   What you do
Still betters what is done. When you speak, sweet,
I'd have you do it ever; when you sing,
I'd have you buy and sell so, so give alms,
Pray so; and for the ord'ring your affairs,
To sing them too. When you do dance, I wish you
A wave o'th' sea, that you might ever do
Nothing but that, move still, still so,
And own no other function. Each your doing,
So singular in each particular,
Crowns what you are doing in the present deeds,
That all your acts are queens.

                              (The Winter's Tale, 4.4.112–46)

An English King Woos a French Princess

Having conquered France, Henry V of England woos Catherine, the French princess.

KING HARRY Fair Catherine, and most fair,
Will you vouchsafe to teach a soldier terms
Such as will enter at a lady's ear
And plead his love-suit to her gentle heart?

CATHERINE Your majesty shall mock at me. I cannot speak your England.

KING HARRY O fair Catherine, if you will love me soundly with your French heart, I will be glad to hear you confess it brokenly with your English tongue. Do you like me, Kate?

CATHERINE *Pardonnez-moi*, I cannot tell vat is 'like me'.

KING HARRY An angel is like you, Kate, and you are like an angel.

CATHERINE (*to Alice, her gentlewoman*) *Que dit-il?—que je suis semblable à les anges?*

ALICE *Oui, vraiment—sauf votre grâce—ainsi dit-il.*

KING HARRY I said so, dear Catherine, and I must not blush to affirm it.

CATHERINE *O bon Dieu! Les langues des hommes sont pleines de tromperies.*

KING HARRY What says she, fair one? That the tongues of men are full of deceits?

ALICE *Oui*, dat de tongeus of de mans is be full of deceits—dat is de Princess.

KING HARRY The Princess is the better Englishwoman. I'faith, Kate, my wooing is fit for thy understanding. I am glad thou canst speak no better English, for if thou couldst, thou wouldst find me such a plain king that thou wouldst think I had sold my farm to buy my crown. I know no ways to mince it in love, but directly to say, 'I love you'; then if you urge me farther than to say, 'Do you in faith?', I wear out my suit. Give me your answer, i'faith do, and so clap hands and a bargain. How say you, lady?

CATHERINE *Sauf votre honneur*, me understand well.

KING HARRY Marry, if you would put me to verses, or to dance for your sake, Kate, why, you undid me. For the one I have neither words nor measure, and for the other I have no strength in measure—yet a reasonable measure in strength. If I could win a lady at leap-frog, or by vaulting into my saddle with my armour on my back, under the correction of bragging be it spoken, I should quickly leap into a wife. Or if I might buffet for my love, or bound my horse for her favours, I could lay on like a butcher, and sit like a jackanapes, never off. But before God, Kate, I cannot look greenly, nor gasp out my eloquence, nor I have no cunning in protestation—only downright oaths, which I never use till urged, nor never break for urging. If thou canst love a fellow of this temper, Kate, whose face is not worth sunburning, that never looks in his glass for love of anything he sees there, let thine eye be thy cook. I speak to thee plain soldier: if thou canst love me for this, take me. If not, to say to thee that I shall die, is true—but for thy love, by the Lord, no. Yet I love thee, too. And while thou livest, dear Kate, take a fellow of plain and uncoined constancy, for he perforce must do thee right, because he hath not the gift to woo in other places. For these fellows of infinite tongue, that can rhyme themselves into ladies' favours, they do always reason themselves out again. What! A speaker is but a prater, a rhyme is but a ballad; a good leg will fall, a straight back will stoop, a black beard will turn white, a curled pate will grow bald, a fair face will wither, a full eye will wax hollow, but a good heart, Kate, is the sun and the moon—or rather the sun and not the moon, for it shines bright and never changes, but keeps his course truly. If thou would have such a one, take me; and take me, take a soldier; take a soldier, take a king. And what sayst thou then to my love? Speak, my fair—and fairly, I pray thee.

CATHERINE Is it possible dat I sould love de *ennemi* of France?

KING HARRY No, it is not possible you should love the enemy of France, Kate. But in loving me, you should love the friend of France, for I love France so well that I will not part with a village of it, I will have it all mine; and Kate, when France is mine, and I am yours, then yours is France, and you are mine.

CATHERINE I cannot tell vat is dat.

KING HARRY No, Kate? I will tell thee in French—which I am sure will hang upon my tongue like a new-married wife about her husband's neck, hardly to be shook off. *Je quand suis le possesseur de France, et quand vous avez le possession de moi*—let me see, what then? Saint Denis be my speed!—*donc vôtre est France, et vous êtes mienne*. It is as easy for me, Kate, to conquer the kingdom as to speak so much more French. I shall never move thee in French, unless it be to laugh at me.

CATHERINE *Sauf votre honneur, le français que vous parlez, il est meilleur que l'anglais lequel je parle*.

KING HARRY No, faith, is't not, Kate. But thy speaking of my tongue, and I thine, most truly-falsely, must needs be granted to be much at one. But Kate, dost thou understand thus much English? Canst thou love me?

CATHERINE I cannot tell.

KING HARRY Can any of your neighbours tell, Kate? I'll ask them. Come, I know thou lovest me, and at night when you come into your closet you'll question this gentlewoman about me, and I know, Kate, you will to her dispraise those parts in me that you love with your heart. But good Kate, mock me mercifully—the rather, gentle princess, because I love thee cruelly. If ever thou be'st mine, Kate—as I have a saving faith within me tells me thou shalt—I get thee with scrambling, and thou must therefore needs prove a good soldier-breeder. Shall not thou and I, between Saint Denis and Saint George, compound a boy, half-French half-English, that shall go to Constantinople and take the Turk by the beard? Shall we not? What sayst thou, my fair flower-de-luce?

CATHERINE I do not know dat.

KING HARRY No, 'tis hereafter to know, but now to promise. Do but now promise, Kate, you will endeavour for your French part of such a boy, and for my English moiety take the word of a king and a bachelor. How answer you, *la plus belle Catherine du monde, mon très chère et divine déesse?*

CATHERINE Your *majesté* 'ave *faux* French enough to deceive de most sage *demoiselle* dat is *en France.*

KING HARRY Now fie upon my false French! By mine honour, in true English, I love thee, Kate. By which honour I dare not swear thou lovest me, yet my blood begins to flatter me that thou dost, notwithstanding the poor and untempering effect of my visage. Now beshrew my father's ambition! He was thinking of civil wars when he got me; therefore was I created with a stubborn outside, with an aspect of iron, that when I come to woo ladies I fright them. But in faith, Kate, the elder I wax the better I shall appear. My comfort is that old age, that ill layer-up of beauty, can do no more spoil upon my face. Thou hast me, if thou hast me, at the worst, and thou shalt wear me, if thou wear me, better and better; and therefore tell me, most fair Catherine, will you have me? Put off your maiden blushes, avouch the thoughts of your heart with the looks of an empress, take me by the hand and say, 'Harry of England, I am thine'—which word thou shalt no sooner bless mine ear withal, but I will tell thee aloud, 'England is thine, Ireland is thine, France is thine, and Henry Plantagenet is thine'—who, though I speak it before his face, if he be not fellow with the best king, thou shalt find the best king of good fellows. Come, your answer in broken music—for thy voice is music and thy English broken. Therefore, queen of all, Catherine, break thy mind to me in broken English: wilt thou have me?

CATHERINE Dat is as it shall please de *roi mon père.*

KING HARRY Nay, it will please him well, Kate. It shall please him, Kate.

CATHERINE Den it sall also content me.

KING HARRY Upon that I kiss your hand, and I call you my queen.

CATHERINE *Laissez, mon seigneur, laissez, laissez! Ma foi, je ne veux point que vous abbaissez votre grandeur en baisant la main d'une de votre seigneurie indigne serviteur. Excusez-mois, je vous supplie, mon treis-puissant seigneur.*

KING HARRY Then I will kiss your lips, Kate.

CATHERINE *Les dames et demoiselles pour être baisées devant leurs noces, il n'est pas la coutume de France.*

KING HARRY *(to Alice)* Madam my interpreter, what says she?

ALICE Dat it is not be de *façon pour les* ladies of France—I cannot tell vat is *baiser en* Anglish.

KING HARRY To kiss.

ALICE Your *majesté entend* bettre *que moi.*

KING HARRY It is not a fashion for the maids in France to kiss before they are married, would she say?

ALICE *Oui, vraiment.*

KING HARRY O Kate, nice customs curtsy to great kings. Dear Kate, you and I cannot be confined within the weak list of a country's fashion. We are the makers of manners, Kate, and the liberty that follows our places stops the mouth of all find-faults, as I will do yours, for upholding the nice fashion of your country in denying me a kiss. Therefore, patiently and yielding. *(He kisses her)* You have witchcraft in your lips, Kate. There is more eloquence in a sugar touch of them than in the tongues of the French Council, and they should sooner persuade Harry of England than a general petition of monarchs.

(Henry V, 5.2.98–278)

A Round Unvarnished Tale of Courtship

*Othello justifies his elopement with Brabanzio's daughter Desdemona
before the Duke and Senators of Venice.*

OTHELLO
Most potent, grave, and reverend signors,
My very noble and approved good masters,
That I have ta'en away this old man's daughter,
It is most true, true I have married her.
The very head and front of my offending
Hath this extent, no more. Rude am I in my speech,
And little blessed with the soft phrase of peace,
For since these arms of mine had seven years' pith
Till now some nine moons wasted, they have used
Their dearest action in the tented field,
And little of this great world can I speak
More than pertains to feats of broils and battle.
And therefore little shall I grace my cause
In speaking for myself. Yet, by your gracious patience,
I will a round unvarnished tale deliver
Of my whole course of love, what drugs, what charms,
What conjuration and what mighty magic—
For such proceeding I am charged withal—
I won his daughter.
BRABANZIO   A maiden never bold,

Of spirit so still and quiet that her motion
Blushed at herself—and she in spite of nature,
Of years, of country, credit, everything,
To fall in love with what she feared to look on!
It is a judgement maimed and most imperfect
That will confess perfection so could err
Against all rules of nature, and must be driven
To find out practices of cunning hell
Why this should be. I therefore vouch again
That with some mixtures powerful o'er the blood,
Or with some dram conjured to this effect,
He wrought upon her.

DUKE   To vouch this is no proof
Without more wider and more overt test
Than these thin habits and poor likelihoods
Of modern seeming do prefer against him.

A SENATOR But Othello, speak.
Did you by indirect and forcèd courses
Subdue and poison this young maid's affections,
Or came it by request and such fair question
As soul to soul affordeth?

OTHELLO   I do beseech you,
Send for the lady to the Sagittary,
And let her speak of me before her father.
If you do find me foul in her report,
The trust, the office I do hold of you
Not only take away, but let your sentence
Even fall upon my life.

DUKE (*to officers*)   Fetch Desdemona hither.

OTHELLO

    Ensign, conduct them. You best know the place.

                          Exit Iago with two or three officers

    And till she come, as truly as to heaven

    I do confess the vices of my blood,

    So justly to your grave ears I'll present

    How I did thrive in this fair lady's love,

    And she in mine.

DUKE   Say it, Othello.

OTHELLO

    Her father loved me, oft invited me,

    Still questioned me the story of my life

    From year to year, the battles, sieges, fortunes

    That I have passed.

    I ran it through even from my boyish days

    To th' very moment that he bade me tell it,

    Wherein I spoke of most disastrous chances,

    Of moving accidents by flood and field,

    Of hair-breadth scapes i'th' imminent deadly breach,

    Of being taken by the insolent foe

    And sold to slavery, of my redemption thence,

    And portance in my traveller's history,

    Wherein of antres vast and deserts idle,

    Rough quarries, rocks, and hills whose heads touch
        heaven,

    It was my hint to speak. Such was my process,

    And of the cannibals that each other eat,

    The Anthropophagi, and men whose heads

    Do grow beneath their shoulders. These things to hear

Would Desdemona seriously incline,
But still the house affairs would draw her thence,
Which ever as she could with haste dispatch
She'd come again, and with a greedy ear
Devour up my discourse; which I observing,
Took once a pliant hour, and found good means
To draw from her a prayer of earnest heart
That I would all my pilgrimage dilate,
Whereof by parcels she had something heard,
But not intentively. I did consent,
And often did beguile her of her tears
When I did speak of some distressful stroke
That my youth suffered. My story being done,
She gave me for my pains a world of kisses.
She swore in faith 'twas strange, 'twas passing strange,
'Twas pitiful, 'twas wondrous pitiful,
She wished she had not heard it, yet she wished
That heaven had made her such a man. She thankèd me,
And bade me, if I had a friend that loved her,
I should but teach him how to tell my story,
And that would woo her. Upon this hint I spake.
She loved me for the dangers I had passed,
And I loved her that she did pity them.
This only is the witchcraft I have used.

(*Othello*, 1.3.76–168)

A Lover's Impatience

Juliet awaits news of her lover, Romeo.

JULIET

The clock struck nine when I did send the Nurse.
In half an hour she promised to return.
Perchance she cannot meet him. That's not so.
O, she is lame! Love's heralds should be thoughts,
Which ten times faster glides than the sun's beams
Driving back shadows over louring hills.
Therefore do nimble-pinioned doves draw Love,
And therefore hath the wind-swift Cupid wings.
Now is the sun upon the highmost hill
Of this day's journey, and from nine till twelve
Is three long hours, yet she is not come.
Had she affections and warm youthful blood
She would be as swift in motion as a ball.
My words would bandy her to my sweet love,
And his to me.
But old folks, many feign as they were dead—
Unwieldy, slow, heavy, and pale as lead.

> *Enter the Nurse and Peter*

O God, she comes! O honey Nurse, what news?
Hast thou met with him? Send thy man away.
NURSE Peter, stay at the gate.

> *Exit Peter*

JULIET

Now, good sweet Nurse—O Lord, why look'st thou sad?
Though news be sad, yet tell them merrily;
If good, thou sham'st the music of sweet news
By playing it to me with so sour a face.

NURSE

I am a-weary. Give me leave a while.
Fie, how my bones ache. What a jaunce have I!

JULIET

I would thou hadst my bones and I thy news.
Nay, come, I pray thee speak, good, good Nurse, speak.

NURSE

Jesu, what haste! Can you not stay a while?
Do you not see that I am out of breath?

JULIET

How art thou out of breath when thou hast breath
To say to me that thou art out of breath?
The excuse that thou dost make in this delay
Is longer than the tale thou dost excuse.
Is thy news good or bad? Answer to that.
Say either, and I'll stay the circumstance.
Let me be satisfied: is't good or bad?

NURSE Well, you have made a simple choice. You know not
how to choose a man. Romeo? No, not he; though his face
be better than any man's, yet his leg excels all men's, and
for a hand and a foot and a body, though they be not to be
talked on, yet they are past compare. He is not the flower of
courtesy, but, I'll warrant him, as gentle as a lamb. Go thy
ways, wench. Serve God. What, have you dined at home?

JULIET

No, no. But all this did I know before.

What says he of our marriage—what of that?

NURSE

Lord, how my head aches! What a head have I!

It beats as it would fall in twenty pieces.

My back—

Juliet rubs her back

a' t'other side—ah, my back, my back!

Beshrew your heart for sending me about

To catch my death with jauncing up and down.

JULIET

I'faith, I am sorry that thou art not well.

Sweet, sweet, sweet Nurse, tell me, what says my
love?

NURSE Your love says, like an honest gentleman, and a
courteous, and a kind, and a handsome, and, I warrant, a
virtuous—where is your mother?

JULIET

Where is my mother? Why, she is within.

Where should she be? How oddly thou repliest!

'Your love says like an honest gentleman

"Where is your mother?" '

NURSE   O, God's Lady dear!

Are you so hot? Marry come up, I trow.

Is this the poultice for my aching bones?

Henceforward do your messages yourself.

JULIET

Here's such a coil! Come, what says Romeo?

NURSE

Have you got leave to go to shrift today?

JULIET I have.

NURSE

Then hie you hence to Friar Laurence' cell.
There stays a husband to make you a wife.
Now comes the wanton blood up in your cheeks.
They'll be in scarlet straight at any news.
Hie you to church. I must another way,
To fetch a ladder by the which your love
Must climb a bird's nest soon, when it is dark.
I am the drudge, and toil in your delight,
But you shall bear the burden soon at night.
Go, I'll to dinner. Hie you to the cell.

JULIET

Hie to high fortune! Honest Nurse, farewell.

Exeunt severally

(Romeo and Juliet, 2.4)

An Invocation

Juliet looks eagerly forward to the consummation of her marriage to Romeo.

JULIET

    Gallop apace, you fiery-footed steeds,
    Towards Phoebus' lodging. Such a waggoner
    As Phaëton would whip you to the west
    And bring in cloudy night immediately.
    Spread thy close curtain, love-performing night,
    That runaways' eyes may wink, and Romeo
    Leap to these arms untalked of and unseen.
    Lovers can see to do their amorous rites
    By their own beauties; or, if love be blind,
    It best agrees with night. Come, civil night,
    Thou sober-suited matron all in black,
    And learn me how to lose a winning match
    Played for a pair of stainless maidenhoods.
    Hood my unmanned blood, bating in my cheeks,
    With thy black mantle till strange love grown bold
    Think true love acted simple modesty.
    Come night, come Romeo; come, thou day in night,
    For thou wilt lie upon the wings of night
    Whiter than new snow on a raven's back.
    Come, gentle night; come, loving, black-browed night,
    Give me my Romeo, and when I shall die

Take him and cut him out in little stars,
And he will make the face of heaven so fine
That all the world will be in love with night
And pay no worship to the garish sun.
O, I have bought the mansion of a love
But not possessed it, and though I am sold,
Not yet enjoyed. So tedious is this day
As is the night before some festival
To an impatient child that hath new robes
And may not wear them.

(Romeo and Juliet, 3.2.1–31)

A Lover's Expectation

Troilus waits for Pandarus to bring Cressida to him.

TROILUS

I am giddy. Expectation whirls me round.
Th'imaginary relish is so sweet
That it enchants my sense. What will it be
When that the wat'ry palates taste indeed
Love's thrice-repurèd nectar? Death, I fear me,
Swooning destruction, or some joy too fine,
Too subtle-potent, tuned too sharp in sweetness
For the capacity of my ruder powers.
I fear it much, and I do fear besides
That I shall lose distinction in my joys,
As doth a battle when they charge on heaps
The enemy flying.

(Troilus and Cressida, 3.2.16–27)

Dying for Love

Orlando has told Rosalind (in her disguise as Ganymede) that he will die for love of the true Rosalind.

ROSALIND ... The poor world is almost six thousand years old, and in all this time there was not any man died in his own person, videlicet, in a love-cause. Troilus had his brains dashed out with a Grecian club, yet he did what he could to die before, and he is one of the patterns of love. Leander, he would have lived many a fair year though Hero had turned nun if it had not been for a hot midsummer night, for, good youth, he went but forth to wash him in the Hellespont and, being taken with the cramp, was drowned; and the foolish chroniclers of that age found it was Hero of Sestos. But these are all lies. Men have died from time to time, and worms have eaten them, but not for love.

(As You Like It, 4.1.88–101)

'In such a night . . .'

After their elopement, Shylock's daughter Jessica and Lorenzo have found a welcome at Belmont.

LORENZO
> The moon shines bright. In such a night as this,
> When the sweet wind did gently kiss the trees
> And they did make no noise—in such a night
> Troilus, methinks, mounted the Trojan walls,
> And sighed his soul toward the Grecian tents
> Where Cressid lay that night.

JESSICA   In such a night
> Did Thisbe fearfully o'ertrip the dew
> And saw the lion's shadow ere himself,
> And ran dismayed away.

LORENZO   In such a night
> Stood Dido with a willow in her hand
> Upon the wild sea banks, and waft her love
> To come again to Carthage.

JESSICA   In such a night
> Medea gatherèd the enchanted herbs
> That did renew old Aeson.

LORENZO   In such a night
> Did Jessica steal from the wealthy Jew,
> And with an unthrift love did run from Venice
> As far as Belmont.

JESSICA   In such a night
      Did young Lorenzo swear he loved her well,
      Stealing her soul with many vows of faith,
      And ne'er a true one.

LORENZO   In such a night
      Did pretty Jessica, like a little shrew,
      Slander her love, and he forgave it her.

                              (*The Merchant of Venice*, 5.1.1–22)

Lovers' Vows

In the presence of Cressida's uncle, Pandarus, who has brought them together, Troilus and Cressida vow to be faithful.

TROILUS

O that I thought it could be in a woman—
As, if it can, I will presume in you—
To feed for aye her lamp and flames of love,
To keep her constancy in plight and youth,
Outliving beauty's outward, with a mind
That doth renew swifter than blood decays;
Or that persuasion could but thus convince me
That my integrity and truth to you
Might be affronted with the match and weight
Of such a winnowed purity in love.
How were I then uplifted! But alas,
I am as true as truth's simplicity,
And simpler than the infancy of truth.

CRESSIDA

In that I'll war with you.

TROILUS   O virtuous fight,
When right with right wars who shall be most right.
True swains in love shall in the world to come
Approve their truth by Troilus. When their rhymes,
Full of protest, of oath and big compare,
Wants similes, truth tired with iteration—

'As true as steel, as plantage to the moon,
As sun to day, as turtle to her mate,
As iron to adamant, as earth to th' centre'—
Yet, after all comparisons of truth,
As truth's authentic author to be cited,
'As true as Troilus' shall crown up the verse
And sanctify the numbers.

CRESSIDA   Prophet may you be!
If I be false, or swerve a hair from truth,
When time is old and hath forgot itself,
When water drops have worn the stones of Troy
And blind oblivion swallowed cities up,
And mighty states characterless are grated
To dusty nothing, yet let memory
From false to false among false maids in love
Upbraid my falsehood. When they've said, 'as false
As air, as water, wind or sandy earth,
As fox to lamb, or wolf to heifer's calf,
Pard to the hind, or stepdame to her son',
Yea, let them say, to stick the heart of falsehood,
'As false as Cressid'.

PANDARUS Go to, a bargain made. Seal it, seal it. I'll be the
witness. Here I hold your hand; here, my cousin's. If ever
you prove false one to another, since I have taken such pain
to bring you together, let all pitiful goers-between be called
to the world's end after my name: call them all panders. Let
all constant men be Troiluses, all false women Cressids, and
all brokers-between panders. Say 'Amen'.

TROILUS Amen.

CRESSIDA Amen.

PANDARUS Amen. Whereupon I will show you a chamber with a bed—which bed, because it shall not speak of your pretty encounters, press it to death. Away!

Exeunt Troilus and Cressida

And Cupid grant all tongue-tied maidens here
Bed, chamber, pander to provide this gear. *Exit*

(Troilus and Cressida, 3.2.154–207)

Lovers' Parting

Pisanio tells Innogen how Posthumus, his master and her husband, banished by Cymbeline, her father, sailed away from Milford - Haven.

INNOGEN

    I would thou grew'st unto the shores o'th' haven
    And questionedst every sail. If he should write
    And I not have it, 'twere a paper lost
    As offered mercy is. What was the last
    That he spake to thee?

PISANIO   It was his queen, his queen.

INNOGEN

    Then waved his handkerchief?

PISANIO   And kissed it, madam.

INNOGEN

    Senseless linen, happier therein than I!
    And that was all?

PISANIO   No, madam. For so long
    As he could make me with this eye or ear
    Distinguish him from others he did keep
    The deck, with glove or hat or handkerchief
    Still waving, as the fits and stirs of 's mind
    Could best express how slow his soul sailed on,
    How swift his ship.

INNOGEN   Thou shouldst have made him

As little as a crow, or less, ere left
To after-eye him.

PISANIO   Madam, so I did.

INNOGEN

I would have broke mine eye-strings, cracked them, but
To look upon him till the diminution
Of space had pointed him sharp as my needle;
Nay, followed him till he had melted from
The smallness of a gnat to air, and then
Have turned mine eye and wept.

(Cymbeline, 1.3.1–22)

A Dawn Parting (1)

Romeo, banished, parts from Juliet on their wedding night.

JULIET

Wilt thou be gone? It is not yet near day.
It was the nightingale, and not the lark,
That pierced the fear-full hollow of thine ear.
Nightly she sings on yon pom'granate tree.
Believe me, love, it was the nightingale.

ROMEO

It was the lark, the herald of the morn,
No nightingale. Look, love, what envious streaks
Do lace the severing clouds in yonder east.
Night's candles are burnt out, and jocund day
Stands tiptoe on the misty mountain tops.
I must be gone and live, or stay and die.

JULIET

Yon light is not daylight; I know it, I.
It is some meteor that the sun exhaled
To be to thee this night a torchbearer
And light thee on thy way to Mantua.
Therefore stay yet. Thou need'st not to be gone.

ROMEO

Let me be ta'en, let me be put to death.
I am content, so thou wilt have it so.
I'll say yon grey is not the morning's eye,

'Tis but the pale reflex of Cynthia's brow;
Nor that is not the lark whose notes do beat
The vaulty heaven so high above our heads.
I have more care to stay than will to go.
Come, death, and welcome; Juliet wills it so.
How is't, my soul? Let's talk. It is not day.

JULIET

It is, it is. Hie hence, be gone, away.
It is the lark that sings so out of tune,
Straining harsh discords and unpleasing sharps.
Some say the lark makes sweet division;
This doth not so, for she divideth us.
Some say the lark and loathèd toad changed eyes.
O, now I would they had changed voices, too,
Since arm from arm that voice doth us affray,
Hunting thee hence with hunt's-up to the day.
O, now be gone! More light and light it grows.

ROMEO

More light and light, more dark and dark our woes.

(Romeo and Juliet, 3.5.1–36)

A Dawn Parting (2)

Troilus parts from Cressida after their first night of love.

TROILUS

    Dear, trouble not yourself. The morn is cold.

CRESSIDA

    Then, sweet my lord, I'll call mine uncle down.

    He shall unbolt the gates.

TROILUS   Trouble him not.

    To bed, to bed! Sleep lull those pretty eyes

    And give as soft attachment to thy senses

    As to infants empty of all thought.

CRESSIDA Good morrow, then.

TROILUS I prithee now, to bed.

CRESSIDA Are you aweary of me?

TROILUS

    O Cressida! But that the busy day,

    Waked by the lark, hath roused the ribald crows,

    And dreaming night will hide our joys no longer,

    I would not from thee.

CRESSIDA   Night hath been too brief.

TROILUS

    Beshrew the witch! With venomous wights she stays

    As hideously as hell, but flies the grasps of love

    With wings more momentary-swift than thought.

    You will catch cold and curse me.

CRESSIDA Prithee, tarry. You men will never tarry.
    O foolish Cressid! I might have still held off,
    And then you would have tarried.

               (Troilus and Cressida, 4.2.1–20)

Love's Contentment

Desdemona has preceded her newly married husband Othello to Cyprus.

OTHELLO (*to Desdemona*)
    O my fair warrior!
DESDEMONA   My dear Othello.
OTHELLO

    It gives me wonder great as my content
    To see you here before me. O my soul's joy,
    If after every tempest come such calms,
    May the winds blow till they have wakened death,
    And let the labouring barque climb hills of seas
    Olympus-high, and duck again as low
    As hell's from heaven. If it were now to die
    'Twere now to be most happy, for I fear
    My soul hath her content so absolute
    That not another comfort like to this
    Succeeds in unknown fate.
DESDEMONA   The heavens forbid
    But that our loves and comforts should increase
    Even as our days do grow.
OTHELLO   Amen to that, sweet powers!
    I cannot speak enough of this content.
    It stops me here, it is too much of joy.

And this, (*they kiss*) and this, the greatest discords be
That e'er our hearts shall make.

(Othello, 2.1.183–200)

Love's Power

Let me not to the marriage of true minds
Admit impediments. Love is not love
Which alters when it alteration finds,
Or bends with the remover to remove.
O no, it is an ever fixèd mark
That looks on tempests and is never shaken;
It is the star to every wand'ring barque,
Whose worth's unknown although his height be taken.
Love's not time's fool, though rosy lips and cheeks
Within his bending sickle's compass come;
Love alters not with his brief hours and weeks,
But bears it out even to the edge of doom.
  If this be error and upon me proved,
  I never writ, nor no man ever loved.

(Sonnet 116)

Love's Dedication

Portia, the Lady of Belmont, dedicates herself to Bassanio after he has won her hand.

PORTIA

> You see me, Lord Bassanio, where I stand,
> Such as I am. Though for myself alone
> I would not be ambitious in my wish
> To wish myself much better, yet for you
> I would be trebled twenty times myself,
> A thousand times more fair, ten thousand times more
>   rich,
> That only to stand high in your account
> I might in virtues, beauties, livings, friends,
> Exceed account. But the full sum of me
> Is sum of something which, to term in gross,
> Is an unlessoned girl, unschooled, unpractisèd,
> Happy in this, she is not yet so old
> But she may learn; happier than this,
> She is not bred so dull but she can learn;
> Happiest of all is that her gentle spirit
> Commits itself to yours to be directed
> As from her lord, her governor, her king.
> Myself and what is mine to you and yours
> Is now converted. But now I was the lord
> Of this fair mansion, master of my servants,

Queen o'er myself; and even now, but now,
This house, these servants, and this same myself
Are yours, my lord's. I give them with this ring,
Which when you part from, lose, or give away,
Let it presage the ruin of your love,
And be my vantage to exclaim on you.

(*The Merchant of Venice*, 3.2.149–74)

A Wife's Duty

Petruccio tells his once-shrewish wife Katherine to instruct her sister Bianca, and the widow whom his friend Hortensio has married, in the duties of a wife.

PETRUCCIO

    Katherine, I charge thee tell these headstrong women
    What duty they do owe their lords and husbands.

WIDOW

    Come, come, you're mocking. We will have no telling.

PETRUCCIO

    Come on, I say, and first begin with her.

WIDOW She shall not.

PETRUCCIO

    I say she shall: and first begin with her.

KATHERINE

    Fie, fie, unknit that threat'ning, unkind brow,
    And dart not scornful glances from those eyes
    To wound thy lord, thy king, thy governor.
    It blots thy beauty as frosts do bite the meads,
    Confounds thy fame as whirlwinds shake fair buds,
    And in no sense is meet or amiable.
    A woman moved is like a fountain troubled,
    Muddy, ill-seeming, thick, bereft of beauty,
    And while it is so, none so dry or thirsty
    Will deign to sip or touch one drop of it.

Thy husband is thy lord, thy life, thy keeper,
Thy head, thy sovereign, one that cares for thee,
And for thy maintenance commits his body
To painful labour both by sea and land,
To watch the night in storms, the day in cold,
Whilst thou liest warm at home, secure and safe,
And craves no other tribute at thy hands
But love, fair looks, and true obedience,
Too little payment for so great a debt.
Such duty as the subject owes the prince,
Even such a woman oweth to her husband,
And when she is froward, peevish, sullen, sour,
And not obedient to his honest will,
What is she but a foul contending rebel,
And graceless traitor to her loving lord?
I am ashamed that women are so simple
To offer war where they should kneel for peace,
Or seek for rule, supremacy, and sway
When they are bound to serve, love, and obey.
Why are our bodies soft, and weak, and smooth,
Unapt to toil and trouble in the world,
But that our soft conditions and our hearts
Should well agree with our external parts?
Come, come, you froward and unable worms,
My mind hath been as big as one of yours,
My heart as great, my reason haply more,
To bandy word for word and frown for frown;
But now I see our lances are but straws,
Our strength as weak, our weakness past compare,

That seeming to be most which we indeed least are.
Then vail your stomachs, for it is no boot,
And place your hands below your husband's foot,
In token of which duty, if he please,
My hand is ready, may it do him ease.

PETRUCCIO

Why, there's a wench! Come on, and kiss me, Kate.
They kiss

(*The Taming of the Shrew*, 5.2.135–85)

A Family Parting

Lance and his dog are to accompany his master Proteus on a journey.

Enter Lance with his dog Crab

LANCE *(to the audience)* Nay, 'twill be this hour ere I have done weeping. All the kind of the Lances have this very fault. I have received my proportion, like the prodigious son, and am going with Sir Proteus to the Imperial's court. I think Crab, my dog, be the sourest-natured dog that lives. My mother weeping, my father wailing, my sister crying, our maid howling, our cat wringing her hands, and all our house in a great perplexity, yet did not this cruel-hearted cur shed one tear. He is a stone, a very pebble-stone, and has no more pity in him than a dog. A Jew would have wept to have seen our parting. Why, my grandam, having no eyes, look you, wept herself blind at my parting. Nay, I'll show you the manner of it. This shoe is my father. No, this left shoe is my father. No, no, this left shoe is my mother. Nay, that cannot be so, neither. Yes, it is so, it is so, it hath the worser sole. This shoe with the hole in it is my mother, and this my father. A vengeance on't, there 'tis. Now, sir, this staff is my sister, for, look you, she is as white as a lily and as small as a wand. This hat is Nan our maid. I am the dog. No, the dog is himself, and I am the dog. O, the dog is me, and I am myself. Ay, so, so. Now come I to my father. 'Father, your blessing.' Now should not the shoe speak a word for weeping. Now should I kiss my father. Well, he weeps on. Now come I to my mother. O that she could speak now, like a moved woman. Well, I kiss her. Why, there 'tis. Here's my mother's breath up and down. Now come I to my sister. Mark the moan she makes.—Now the dog all this while sheds not a tear nor speaks a word. But see how I lay the dust with my tears.

(The Two Gentlemen of Verona, 2.3.1–32)

A Daughter Begets a Father

In a storm at sea Thaisa, wife of Pericles, Prince of Tyre, apparently died giving birth to a daughter, Marina (see pp. 344–7). Misinformed that Marina, grown to womanhood, has been murdered by Cleon and Dionyza—in whose care he left her—Pericles, suffering a depression so profound that he has neither spoken nor eaten for three months, arrives at Mytilene under the care of Lord Helicanus. There the governor, Lysimachus, brings Marina (of whose parentage he is unaware) aboard Pericles' ship in the hope that her presence will restore him; she does not know who he is.

MARINA *(to Pericles)*
    Hail, sir; my lord, lend ear.
PERICLES Hmh, ha!
       He roughly repulses her
MARINA   I am a maid,
    My lord, that ne'er before invited eyes,
    But have been gazed on like a comet. She speaks,
    My lord, that maybe hath endured a grief
    Might equal yours, if both were justly weighed.
    Though wayward fortune did malign my state,
    My derivation was from ancestors
    Who stood equivalent with mighty kings,
    But time hath rooted out my parentage,
    And to the world and awkward casualties
    Bound me in servitude. *(Aside)* I will desist.

But there is something glows upon my cheek,
And whispers in mine ear 'Stay till he speak.'

PERICLES

My fortunes, parentage, good parentage,
To equal mine? Was it not thus? What say you?

MARINA

I said if you did know my parentage,
My lord, you would not do me violence.

PERICLES

I do think so. Pray you, turn your eyes upon me.
You're like something that—what countrywoman?
Here of these shores?

MARINA   No, nor of any shores,
Yet I was mortally brought forth, and am
No other than I seem.

PERICLES (*aside*)

I am great with woe, and shall deliver weeping.
My dearest wife was like this maid, and such
My daughter might have been. My queen's square
    brows,
Her stature to an inch, as wand-like straight,
As silver-voiced, her eyes as jewel-like,
And cased as richly, in pace another Juno,
Who starves the ears she feeds, and makes them hungry
The more she gives them speech.—Where do you live?

MARINA

Where I am but a stranger. From the deck
You may discern the place.

PERICLES   Where were you bred,

And how achieved you these endowments which
You make more rich to owe?

MARINA   If I should tell
My history, it would seem like lies
Disdained in the reporting.

PERICLES   Prithee speak.
Falseness cannot come from thee, for thou look'st
Modest as justice, and thou seem'st a palace
For the crowned truth to dwell in. I will believe thee,
And make my senses credit thy relation
To points that seem impossible. Thou show'st
Like one I loved indeed. What were thy friends?
Didst thou not say, when I did push thee back—
Which was when I perceived thee—that thou cam'st
From good descending?

MARINA   So indeed I did.

PERICLES
Report thy parentage. I think thou said'st
Thou hadst been tossed from wrong to injury,
And that thou thought'st thy griefs might equal mine,
If both were opened.

MARINA   Some such thing I said,
And said no more but what my circumstance
Did warrant me was likely.

PERICLES   Tell thy story.
If thine considered prove the thousandth part
Of my endurance, thou art a man, and I
Have suffered like a girl. Yet thou dost look
Like patience gazing on kings' graves, and smiling

Extremity out of act. What were thy friends?
How lost thou them? Thy name, my most kind virgin?
Recount, I do beseech thee. Come, sit by me.
>*She sits*

MARINA
My name, sir, is Marina.

PERICLES   O, I am mocked,
And thou by some incensèd god sent hither
To make the world to laugh at me.

MARINA   Patience, good sir,
Or here I'll cease.

PERICLES   Nay, I'll be patient.
Thou little know'st how thou dost startle me
To call thyself Marina.

MARINA   The name
Was given me by one that had some power:
My father, and a king.

PERICLES   How, a king's daughter,
And called Marina?

MARINA   You said you would believe me,
But not to be a troubler of your peace
I will end here.

PERICLES   But are you flesh and blood?
Have you a working pulse and are no fairy?
Motion as well? Speak on. Where were you born,
And wherefore called Marina?

MARINA   Called Marina
For I was born at sea.

PERICLES   At sea? What mother?

MARINA

> My mother was the daughter of a king,
> Who died when I was born, as my good nurse
> Lychorida hath oft recounted weeping.

PERICLES

> O, stop there a little! (*Aside*) This is the rarest dream
> That e'er dulled sleep did mock sad fools withal.
> This cannot be my daughter, buried. Well.
> (*To Marina*) Where were you bred? I'll hear you more to
>   th' bottom
> Of your story, and never interrupt you.

MARINA

> You will scarce believe me. 'Twere best I did give o'er.

PERICLES

> I will believe you by the syllable
> Of what you shall deliver. Yet give me leave.
> How came you in these parts? Where were you bred?

MARINA

> The King my father did in Tarsus leave me,
> Till cruel Cleon, with his wicked wife,
> Did seek to murder me, and wooed a villain
> To attempt the deed; who having drawn to do't,
> A crew of pirates came and rescued me.
> To Mytilene they brought me. But, good sir,
> What will you of me? Why do you weep? It may be
> You think me an impostor. No, good faith,
> I am the daughter to King Pericles,
> If good King Pericles be.

PERICLES (*rising*) Ho, Helicanus!

HELICANUS (*coming forward*) Calls my lord?

PERICLES

    Thou art a grave and noble counsellor,

    Most wise in gen'ral. Tell me if thou canst

    What this maid is, or what is like to be,

    That thus hath made me weep.

HELICANUS   I know not.

    But here's the regent, sir, of Mytilene

    Speaks nobly of her.

LYSIMACHUS   She would never tell

    Her parentage. Being demanded that,

    She would sit still and weep.

PERICLES

    O Helicanus, strike me, honoured sir,

    Give me a gash, put me to present pain,

    Lest this great sea of joys rushing upon me

    O'erbear the shores of my mortality

    And drown me with their sweetness! (*To Marina*) O,

      come hither,

        Marina stands

    Thou that begett'st him that did thee beget,

    Thou that wast born at sea, buried at Tarsus,

    And found at sea again!—O Helicanus,

    Down on thy knees, thank the holy gods as loud

    As thunder threatens us, this is Marina!

    (*To Marina*) What was thy mother's name? Tell me but

      that,

    For truth can never be confirmed enough,

    Though doubts did ever sleep.

MARINA   First, sir, I pray,
    What is your title?
PERICLES   I am Pericles
    Of Tyre. But tell me now my drowned queen's name.
    As in the rest thou hast been godlike perfect,
    So prove but true in that, thou art my daughter,
    The heir of kingdoms, and another life
    To Pericles thy father.
MARINA (*kneeling*)   Is it no more
    To be your daughter than to say my mother's name?
    Thaisa was my mother, who did end
    The minute I began.
PERICLES
    Now blessing on thee! Rise. Thou art my child.
        Marina stands. He kisses her
    (*To attendants*) Give me fresh garments.—Mine own,
        Helicanus!
    Not dead at Tarsus, as she should have been
    By savage Cleon. She shall tell thee all,
    When thou shalt kneel and justify in knowledge
    She is thy very princess. Who is this?
HELICANUS
    Sir, 'tis the governor of Mytilene,
    Who, hearing of your melancholy state,
    Did come to see you.
PERICLES (*to Lysimachus*) I embrace you, sir.—
    Give me my robes.
        He is attired in fresh robes
                        I am wild in my beholding.

O heavens, bless my girl!
> *Celestial music*

                    But hark, what music?
Tell Helicanus, my Marina, tell him
O'er point by point, for yet he seems to doubt,
How sure you are my daughter. But what music?
HELICANUS My lord, I hear none.
PERICLES

None? The music of the spheres! List, my Marina.
LYSIMACHUS *(aside to the others)*

It is not good to cross him. Give him way.
PERICLES Rar'st sounds. Do ye not hear?
LYSIMACHUS Music, my lord?
PERICLES I hear most heav'nly music.
It raps me unto list'ning, and thick slumber
Hangs upon mine eyelids. Let me rest.
> *He sleeps*

LYSIMACHUS

A pillow for his head.
(To Marina and others) Companion friends,
If this but answer to my just belief
I'll well remember you. So leave him all.
>   *Exeunt all but Pericles*
>   (*Pericles*, sc. 21, ll. 71–224)

Reunion and Reconciliation

Cordelia, now Queen of France, meets again her old father, King Lear, who disowned her, and whose sufferings have driven him to madness.

CORDELIA
   . . . How does the King?
FIRST GENTLEMAN   Madam, sleeps still.
CORDELIA   O you kind gods,
   Cure this great breach in his abusèd nature;
   Th'untuned and jarring senses O wind up
   Of this child-changèd father!
FIRST GENTLEMAN   So please your majesty
   That we may wake the King? He hath slept long.
CORDELIA
   Be governed by your knowledge, and proceed
   I'th' sway of your own will. Is he arrayed?
FIRST GENTLEMAN
   Ay, madam. In the heaviness of sleep
   We put fresh garments on him.
      Enter King Lear asleep, in a chair carried by servants
   Be by, good madam, when we do awake him.
   I doubt not of his temperance.
CORDELIA
   O my dear father, restoration hang
   Thy medicine on my lips, and let this kiss

Repair those violent harms that my two sisters
Have in thy reverence made!

KENT   Kind and dear princess!

CORDELIA *(to Lear)*

Had you not been their father, these white flakes
Did challenge pity of them. Was this a face
To be opposed against the warring winds?
Mine enemy's dog, though he had bit me, should have
    stood
That night against my fire. And wast thou fain, poor father,
To hovel thee with swine and rogues forlorn
In short and musty straw? Alack, alack,
'Tis wonder that thy life and wits at once
Had not concluded all! *(To the Gentleman)* He wakes.
    Speak to him.

FIRST GENTLEMAN Madam, do you; 'tis fittest.

CORDELIA *(to Lear)*

How does my royal lord? How fares your majesty?

LEAR

You do me wrong to take me out o'th' grave.
Thou art a soul in bliss, but I am bound
Upon a wheel of fire, that mine own tears
Do scald like molten lead.

CORDELIA   Sir, do you know me?

LEAR

You are a spirit, I know. Where did you die?

CORDELIA *(to the Gentleman)* Still, still far wide!

FIRST GENTLEMAN

He's scarce awake. Let him alone a while.

LEAR

    Where have I been? Where am I? Fair daylight?
    I am mightily abused. I should ev'n die with pity
    To see another thus. I know not what to say.
    I will not swear these are my hands. Let's see:
    I feel this pin prick. Would I were assured
    Of my condition.

CORDELIA *(kneeling)* O look upon me, sir,
    And hold your hands in benediction o'er me.
    You must not kneel.

LEAR   Pray do not mock.
    I am a very foolish, fond old man,
    Fourscore and upward,
    Not an hour more nor less; and to deal plainly,
    I fear I am not in my perfect mind.
    Methinks I should know you, and know this man;
    Yet I am doubtful, for I am mainly ignorant
    What place this is; and all the skill I have
    Remembers not these garments; nor I know not
    Where I did lodge last night. Do not laugh at me,
    For as I am a man, I think this lady
    To be my child, Cordelia.

CORDELIA   And so I am, I am.

LEAR

    Be your tears wet? Yes, faith. I pray, weep not.
    If you have poison for me, I will drink it.
    I know you do not love me; for your sisters
    Have, as I do remember, done me wrong.
    You have some cause; they have not.

CORDELIA   No cause, no cause.

LEAR Am I in France?

KENT In your own kingdom, sir.

LEAR Do not abuse me.

FIRST GENTLEMAN

Be comforted, good madam. The great rage
You see is killed in him. Desire him to go in.
Trouble him no more till further settling.

CORDELIA (*to Lear*) Will't please your highness walk?

LEAR

You must bear with me. Pray you now, forget
And forgive. I am old and foolish.   *Exeunt*

(*The Tragedy of King Lear*, 4.6.12–77)

A Marital Quarrel

Oberon, King of the Fairies, encounters his estranged wife Titania.

OBERON

Ill met by moonlight, proud Titania.

TITANIA

What, jealous Oberon?—Fairies, skip hence.

I have forsworn his bed and company.

OBERON

Tarry, rash wanton. Am not I thy lord?

TITANIA

Then I must be thy lady; but I know

When thou hast stol'n away from fairyland

And in the shape of Corin sat all day,

Playing on pipes of corn, and versing love

To amorous Phillida. Why art thou here

Come from the farthest step of India,

But that, forsooth, the bouncing Amazon,

Your buskined mistress and your warrior love,

To Theseus must be wedded, and you come

To give their bed joy and prosperity?

OBERON

How canst thou thus for shame, Titania,

Glance at my credit with Hippolyta,

Knowing I know thy love to Theseus?

Didst not thou lead him through the glimmering night

From Perigouna whom he ravishèd,
And make him with fair Aegles break his faith,
With Ariadne and Antiopa?

TITANIA

These are the forgeries of jealousy,
And never since the middle summer's spring
Met we on hill, in dale, forest, or mead,
By pavèd fountain or by rushy brook,
Or in the beachèd margin of the sea
To dance our ringlets to the whistling wind,
But with thy brawls thou hast disturbed our sport.
Therefore the winds, piping to us in vain,
As in revenge have sucked up from the sea
Contagious fogs which, falling in the land,
Hath every pelting river made so proud
That they have overborne their continents.
The ox hath therefore stretched his yoke in vain,
The ploughman lost his sweat, and the green corn
Hath rotted ere his youth attained a beard.
The fold stands empty in the drownèd field,
And crows are fatted with the murrain flock.
The nine men's morris is filled up with mud,
And the quaint mazes in the wanton green
For lack of tread are undistinguishable.
The human mortals want their winter cheer.
No night is now with hymn or carol blessed.
Therefore the moon, the governess of floods,
Pale in her anger washes all the air,
That rheumatic diseases do abound;

And thorough this distemperature we see
The seasons alter: hoary-headed frosts
Fall in the fresh lap of the crimson rose,
And on old Hiems' thin and icy crown
An odorous chaplet of sweet summer buds
Is, as in mock'ry, set. The spring, the summer,
The childing autumn, angry winter change
Their wonted liveries, and the mazèd world
By their increase now knows not which is which;
And this same progeny of evils comes
From our debate, from our dissension.
We are their parents and original.

(A Midsummer Night's Dream, 2.1.60–117)

The Consequence of Jealousy

The Abbess censures Adriana's jealous nagging of her husband.

ABBESS

    . . . The venom clamours of a jealous woman
    Poisons more deadly than a mad dog's tooth.
    It seems his sleeps were hindered by thy railing,
    And thereof comes it that his head is light.
    Thou sayst his meat was sauced with thy upbraidings.
    Unquiet meals make ill digestions.
    Thereof the raging fire of fever bred,
    And what's a fever but a fit of madness?
    Thou sayst his sports were hindered by thy brawls.
    Sweet recreation barred, what doth ensue
    But moody and dull melancholy,
    Kinsman to grim and comfortless despair,
    And at her heels a huge infectious troop
    Of pale distemperatures and foes to life?
    In food, in sport, and life-preserving rest
    To be disturbed would mad or man or beast.
    The consequence is, then, thy jealous fits
    Hath scared thy husband from the use of wits.

                (The Comedy of Errors, 5.1.70–87)

The Cuckoo's Threat

SPRING (*sings*)
 When daisies pied and violets blue,
  And lady-smocks, all silver-white,
 And cuckoo-buds of yellow hue
  Do paint the meadows with delight,
 The cuckoo then on every tree
 Mocks married men, for thus sings he:
   Cuckoo!
 Cuckoo, cuckoo—O word of fear,
 Unpleasing to a married ear.

 When shepherds pipe on oaten straws,
  And merry larks are ploughmen's clocks;
 When turtles tread, and rooks and daws,
  And maidens bleach their summer smocks,
 The cuckoo then on every tree
 Mocks married men, for thus sings he:
   Cuckoo!
 Cuckoo, cuckoo—O word of fear,
 Unpleasing to a married ear.

      (*Love's Labour's Lost*, 5.2.880–97)

A Farewell to Love

The warrior Othello, crazed with jealousy, grieves over his lost happiness.

OTHELLO   . . . O, now for ever
  Farewell the tranquil mind, farewell content,
  Farewell the plumèd troops and the big wars
  That makes ambition virtue! O, farewell,
  Farewell the neighing steed and the shrill trump,
  The spirit-stirring drum, th'ear-piercing fife,
  The royal banner, and all quality,
  Pride, pomp, and circumstance of glorious war!
  And O, you mortal engines whose rude throats
  Th'immortal Jove's dread clamours counterfeit,
  Farewell! Othello's occupation's gone.
                              (*Othello*, 3.3.352–62)

Lust in Action

Th'expense of spirit in a waste of shame
Is lust in action; and till action, lust
Is perjured, murd'rous, bloody, full of blame,
Savage, extreme, rude, cruel, not to trust,
Enjoyed no sooner but despisèd straight,
Past reason hunted, and no sooner had
Past reason hated as a swallowed bait
On purpose laid to make the taker mad;
Mad in pursuit and in possession so,
Had, having, and in quest to have, extreme;
A bliss in proof and proved, a very woe;
Before, a joy proposed; behind, a dream.
   All this the world well knows, yet none knows well
   To shun the heaven that leads men to this hell.

(Sonnet 129)

A Lover Ageing

That time of year thou mayst in me behold
When yellow leaves, or none, or few, do hang
Upon those boughs which shake against the cold,
Bare ruined choirs where late the sweet birds sang.
In me thou seest the twilight of such day
As after sunset fadeth in the west,
Which by and by black night doth take away,
Death's second self, that seals up all in rest.
In me thou seest the glowing of such fire
That on the ashes of his youth doth lie
As the death-bed whereon it must expire,
Consumed with that which it was nourished by.
   This thou perceiv'st, which makes thy love more strong,
   To love that well which thou must leave ere long.

(Sonnet 73)

The Phoenix and Turtle

Let the bird of loudest lay
On the sole Arabian tree
Herald sad and trumpet be,
To whose sound chaste wings obey.

But thou shrieking harbinger,
Foul precurrer of the fiend,
Augur of the fever's end—
To this troupe come thou not near.

From this session interdict
Every fowl of tyrant wing
Save the eagle, feathered king.
Keep the obsequy so strict.

Let the priest in surplice white
That defunctive music can,
Be the death-divining swan,
Lest the requiem lack his right.

And thou treble-dated crow,
That thy sable gender mak'st
With the breath thou giv'st and tak'st,
'Mongst our mourners shalt thou go.

Here the anthem doth commence:
Love and constancy is dead,
Phoenix and the turtle fled
In a mutual flame from hence.

So they loved as love in twain
Had the essence but in one,
Two distincts, division none.
Number there in love was slain.

Hearts remote yet not asunder,
Distance and no space was seen
'Twixt this turtle and his queen.
But in them it were a wonder.

So between them love did shine
That the turtle saw his right
Flaming in the Phoenix' sight.
Either was the other's mine.

Property was thus appalled
That the self was not the same.
Single nature's double name
Neither two nor one was called.

Reason, in itself confounded,
Saw division grow together
To themselves, yet either neither,
Simple were so well compounded

That it cried 'How true a twain
Seemeth this concordant one!
Love hath reason, reason none,
If what parts can so remain.'

Whereupon it made this threne
To the phoenix and the dove,
Co-supremes and stars of love,
As chorus to their tragic scene.

Threnos

Beauty, truth, and rarity,
Grace in all simplicity,
Here enclosed in cinders lie.

Death is now the phoenix' nest,
And the turtle's loyal breast
To eternity doth rest.

Leaving no posterity
'Twas not their infirmity,
It was married chastity.

Truth may seem but cannot be,
Beauty brag, but 'tis not she.
Truth and beauty buried be.

To this urn let those repair
That are either true or fair.
For these dead birds sigh a prayer.

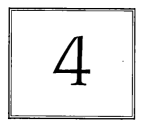

Hatred

A Villain's Creed

The villainous Aaron, faced with death, disclaims penitence.

AARON

. . . Even now I curse the day—and yet I think
Few come within the compass of my curse—
Wherein I did not some notorious ill,
As kill a man, or else devise his death;
Ravish a maid, or plot the way to do it;
Accuse some innocent and forswear myself;
Set deadly enmity between two friends;
Make poor men's cattle break their necks;
Set fire on barns and haystacks in the night,
And bid the owners quench them with their tears.
Oft have I digged up dead men from their graves
And set them upright at their dear friends' door,
Even when their sorrows almost was forgot,
And on their skins, as on the bark of trees,
Have with my knife carvèd in Roman letters
'Let not your sorrow die though I am dead.'
But I have done a thousand dreadful things
As willingly as one would kill a fly,
And nothing grieves me heartily indeed
But that I cannot do ten thousand more.

(*Titus Andronicus*, 5.1.125–44)

Desire for Revenge

Shylock, the Jewish usurer, declares his determination to exact revenge from his enemy, the Christian Antonio.

SHYLOCK . . . He hath disgraced me, and hindered me half a million; laughed at my losses, mocked at my gains, scorned my nation, thwarted my bargains, cooled my friends, heated mine enemies, and what's his reason?—I am a Jew. Hath not a Jew eyes? Hath not a Jew hands, organs, dimensions, senses, affections, passions; fed with the same food, hurt with the same weapons, subject to the same diseases, healed by the same means, warmed and cooled by the same winter and summer as a Christian is? If you prick us do we not bleed? If you tickle us do we not laugh? If you poison us do we not die? And if you wrong us shall we not revenge? If we are like you in the rest, we will resemble you in that. If a Jew wrong a Christian, what is his humility? Revenge. If a Christian wrong a Jew, what should his sufferance be by Christian example? Why, revenge. The villainy you teach me I will execute, and it shall go hard but I will better the instruction.

(*The Merchant of Venice*, 3.1.50–68)

A Merry Bond

Before the Venetian court Shylock defends his determination to exact a pound of flesh from Antonio.

SHYLOCK

 . . . You'll ask me why I rather choose to have
A weight of carrion flesh than to receive
Three thousand ducats. I'll not answer that,
But say it is my humour. Is it answered?
What if my house be troubled with a rat,
And I be pleased to give ten thousand ducats
To have it baned? What, are you answered yet?
Some men there are love not a gaping pig,
Some that are mad if they behold a cat,
And others when the bagpipe sings i'th' nose
Cannot contain their urine; for affection,
Mistress of passion, sways it to the mood
Of what it likes or loathes. Now for your answer:
As there is no firm reason to be rendered
Why he cannot abide a gaping pig,
Why he a harmless necessary cat,
Why he a woollen bagpipe, but of force
Must yield to such inevitable shame
As to offend himself being offended,
So can I give no reason, nor I will not,
More than a lodged hate and a certain loathing

I bear Antonio, that I follow thus
A losing suit against him. Are you answered?

BASSANIO

This is no answer, thou unfeeling man,
To excuse the current of thy cruelty.

SHYLOCK

I am not bound to please thee with my answers.

BASSANIO

Do all men kill the things they do not love?

SHYLOCK

Hates any man the thing he would not kill?

BASSANIO

Every offence is not a hate at first.

SHYLOCK

What, wouldst thou have a serpent sting thee twice?

ANTONIO

I pray you think you question with the Jew.
You may as well go stand upon the beach
And bid the main flood bate his usual height;
You may as well use question with the wolf
Why he hath made the ewe bleat for the lamb;
You may as well forbid the mountain pines
To wag their high tops and to make no noise
When they are fretten with the gusts of heaven,
You may as well do anything most hard
As seek to soften that—than which what's harder?—
His Jewish heart. Therefore, I do beseech you,
Make no more offers, use no farther means,

But with all brief and plain conveniency
Let me have judgement and the Jew his will.
BASSANIO (*to Shylock*)
    For thy three thousand ducats here is six.
SHYLOCK
    If every ducat in six thousand ducats
    Were in six parts, and every part a ducat,
    I would not draw them. I would have my bond.
DUKE
    How shalt thou hope for mercy, rend'ring none?
SHYLOCK
    What judgement shall I dread, doing no wrong?
    You have among you many a purchased slave
    Which, like your asses and your dogs and mules,
    You use in abject and in slavish parts
    Because you bought them. Shall I say to you
    'Let them be free, marry them to your heirs.
    Why sweat they under burdens? Let their beds
    Be made as soft as yours, and let their palates
    Be seasoned with such viands.' You will answer
    'The slaves are ours.' So do I answer you.
    The pound of flesh which I demand of him
    Is dearly bought. 'Tis mine, and I will have it.
    If you deny me, fie upon your law:
    There is no force in the decrees of Venice.
    I stand for judgement. Answer: shall I have it?
                  (*The Merchant of Venice*, 4.1.39–102)

A Widow's Curse

*Lady Anne grieves over the body of her father-in-law Henry VI,
murdered by Richard of Gloucester (later Richard III).*

> *Enter gentlemen, bearing the corpse of King Henry the
> Sixth in an open coffin, with halberdiers to guard it,
> Lady Anne being the mourner*

LADY ANNE

Set down, set down your honourable load,
If honour may be shrouded in a hearse,
Whilst I a while obsequiously lament
Th'untimely fall of virtuous Lancaster.
   They set the coffin down
Poor key-cold figure of a holy king,
Pale ashes of the house of Lancaster,
Thou bloodless remnant of that royal blood:
Be it lawful that I invocate thy ghost
To hear the lamentations of poor Anne,
Wife to thy Edward, to thy slaughtered son,
Stabbed by the selfsame hand that made these wounds.
Lo, in these windows that let forth thy life
I pour the helpless balm of my poor eyes.
O cursèd be the hand that made these holes,
Cursèd the blood that let this blood from hence,
Cursèd the heart that had the heart to do it.
More direful hap betide that hated wretch

That makes us wretched by the death of thee
Than I can wish to wolves, to spiders, toads,
Or any creeping venomed thing that lives.
If ever he have child, abortive be it,
Prodigious, and untimely brought to light,
Whose ugly and unnatural aspect
May fright the hopeful mother at the view,
And that be heir to his unhappiness.
If ever he have wife, let her be made
More miserable by the death of him
Than I am made by my young lord and thee.

(*Richard III*, 1.2.1–28)

A Father's Curse

King Lear curses Goneril, the daughter to whom he has given half of his kingdom and who now seeks to reduce his retinue.

LEAR

    . . . Hear, nature; hear, dear goddess, hear:
Suspend thy purpose if thou didst intend
To make this creature fruitful.
Into her womb convey sterility.
Dry up in her the organs of increase,
And from her derogate body never spring
A babe to honour her. If she must teem,
Create her child of spleen, that it may live
And be a thwart disnatured torment to her.
Let it stamp wrinkles in her brow of youth,
With cadent tears fret channels in her cheeks,
Turn all her mother's pains and benefits
To laughter and contempt, that she may feel—
That she may feel
How sharper than a serpent's tooth it is
To have a thankless child.
               (The Tragedy of King Lear, 1.4.254–69)

The Consequences of War

*The Duke of Burgundy implores Henry V of England and Charles VI of
France to make peace.*

BURGUNDY
>   My duty to you both, on equal love,
>   Great Kings of France and England. That I have
>   laboured
>   With all my wits, my pains, and strong endeavours,
>   To bring your most imperial majesties
>   Unto this bar and royal interview,
>   Your mightiness on both parts best can witness.
>   Since, then, my office hath so far prevailed
>   That face to face and royal eye to eye
>   You have congreeted, let it not disgrace me
>   If I demand, before this royal view,
>   What rub or what impediment there is
>   Why that the naked, poor, and mangled peace,
>   Dear nurse of arts, plenties, and joyful births,
>   Should not in this best garden of the world,
>   Our fertile France, put up her lovely visage?
>   Alas, she hath from France too long been chased,
>   And all her husbandry doth lie on heaps,
>   Corrupting in it own fertility.
>   Her vine, the merry cheerer of the heart,
>   Unprunèd dies; her hedges even-plashed

Like prisoners wildly overgrown with hair
Put forth disordered twigs; her fallow leas
The darnel, hemlock, and rank fumitory
Doth root upon, while that the coulter rusts
That should deracinate such savagery.
The even mead—that erst brought sweetly forth
The freckled cowslip, burnet, and green clover—
Wanting the scythe, all uncorrected, rank,
Conceives by idleness, and nothing teems
But hateful docks, rough thistles, kecksies, burs,
Losing both beauty and utility.
An all our vineyards, fallows, meads, and hedges,
Defective in their natures, grow to wildness,
Even so our houses and ourselves and children
Have lost, or do not learn for want of time,
The sciences that should become our country,
But grow like savages—as soldiers will
That nothing do but meditate on blood—
To swearing and stern looks, diffused attire,
And everything that seems unnatural.
Which to reduce into our former favour
You are assembled, and my speech entreats
That I may know the let why gentle peace
Should not expel these inconveniences
And bless us with her former qualities.

(*Henry V*, 5.2.23–67)

A Misanthrope's Curse

The disillusioned Timon curses the city that has betrayed him.

TIMON

Let me look back upon thee. O thou wall
That girdles in those wolves, dive in the earth,
And fence not Athens! Matrons, turn incontinent!
Obedience fail in children! Slaves and fools,
Pluck the grave wrinkled senate from the bench
And minister in their steads! To general filths
Convert o'th' instant, green virginity!
Do't in your parents' eyes. Bankrupts, hold fast!
Rather than render back, out with your knives,
And cut your trusters' throats. Bound servants, steal!
Large-handed robbers your grave masters are,
And pill by law. Maid, to thy master's bed!
Thy mistress is o'th' brothel. Son of sixteen,
Pluck the lined crutch from thy old limping sire;
With it beat out his brains! Piety and fear,
Religion to the gods, peace, justice, truth,
Domestic awe, night rest, and neighbourhood,
Instruction, manners, mysteries, and trades,
Degrees, observances, customs, and laws,
Decline to your confounding contraries,
And let confusion live! Plagues incident to men,
Your potent and infectious fevers heap

On Athens, ripe for stroke! Thou cold sciatica,
Cripple our senators, that their limbs may halt
As lamely as their manners! Lust and liberty,
Creep in the minds and marrows of our youth,
That 'gainst the stream of virtue they may strive
And drown themselves in riot! Itches, blains,
Sow all th'Athenian bosoms, and their crop
Be general leprosy! Breath infect breath,
That their society, as their friendship, may
Be merely poison!

    He tears off his clothes

                  Nothing I'll bear from thee
But nakedness, thou detestable town;
Take thou that too, with multiplying bans.
Timon will to the woods, where he shall find
Th'unkindest beast more kinder than mankind.
The gods confound—hear me you good gods all—
Th'Athenians, both within and out that wall;
And grant, as Timon grows, his hate may grow
To the whole race of mankind, high and low.
Amen.

                    (Timon of Athens, 4.1.1–41)

The Curse of Gold

The impoverished and disillusioned Timon, who has found gold in the woods near Athens, gives it away to thieves.

TIMON   . . . Rascal thieves,
    Here's gold. Go suck the subtle blood o'th' grape
    Till the high fever seethe your blood to froth,
    And so scape hanging. Trust not the physician;
    His antidotes are poison, and he slays
    More than you rob. Take wealth and lives together.
    Do villainy; do, since you protest to do't,
    Like workmen. I'll example you with thievery.
    The sun's a thief, and with his great attraction
    Robs the vast sea. The moon's an arrant thief,
    And her pale fire she snatches from the sun.
    The sea's a thief, whose liquid surge resolves
    The moon into salt tears. The earth's a thief,
    That feeds and breeds by a composture stol'n
    From gen'ral excrement. Each thing's a thief.
    The laws, your curb and whip, in their rough power
    Has unchecked theft. Love not yourselves. Away,
    Rob one another. There's more gold. Cut throats;
    All that you meet are thieves. To Athens go,
    Break open shops; nothing can you steal
    But thieves do lose it. Steal no less for this I give you,
    And gold confound you howsoe'er. Amen.

                     (Timon of Athens, 4.3.430–51)

A Monster's Curse

Caliban curses his master, the magician Prospero.

CALIBAN

All the infections that the sun sucks up
From bogs, fens, flats, on Prosper fall, and make him
By inch-meal a disease!
    A noise of thunder heard
                    His spirits hear me,
And yet I needs must curse. But they'll nor pinch,
Fright me with urchin-shows, pitch me i'th' mire,
Nor lead me like a fire-brand in the dark
Out of my way, unless he bid 'em. But
For every trifle are they set upon me;
Sometime like apes, that mow and chatter at me
And after bite me; then like hedgehogs, which
Lie tumbling in my barefoot way and mount
Their pricks at my footfall; sometime am I
All wound with adders, who with cloven tongues
Do hiss me into madness.

(The Tempest, 2.2.1–14)

Imagination

The Playwright's Plea (1)

The Chorus addresses the audience immediately before a performance of Henry V.

CHORUS
    O for a muse of fire, that would ascend
    The brightest heaven of invention:
    A kingdom for a stage, princes to act,
    And monarchs to behold the swelling scene.
    Then should the warlike Harry, like himself,
    Assume the port of Mars, and at his heels,
    Leashed in like hounds, should famine, sword, and fire
    Crouch for employment. But pardon, gentles all,
    The flat unraisèd spirits that hath dared
    On this unworthy scaffold to bring forth
    So great an object. Can this cock-pit hold
    The vasty fields of France? Or may we cram
    Within this wooden O the very casques
    That did affright the air at Agincourt?
    O pardon: since a crookèd figure may
    Attest in little place a million,
    And let us, ciphers to this great account,
    On your imaginary forces work.
    Suppose within the girdle of these walls
    Are now confined two mighty monarchies,
    Whose high uprearèd and abutting fronts

The perilous narrow ocean parts asunder.
Piece out our imperfections with your thoughts:
Into a thousand parts divide one man,
And make imaginary puissance.
Think, when we talk of horses, that you see them,
Printing their proud hoofs i'th' receiving earth;
For 'tis your thoughts that now must deck our kings,
Carry them here and there, jumping o'er times,
Turning th'accomplishment of many years
Into an hourglass—for the which supply,
Admit me Chorus to this history,
Who Prologue-like your humble patience pray
Gently to hear, kindly to judge, our play.

(*Henry V*, Prologue to Act One)

The Playwright's Plea (2)

The Chorus addresses the audience during a performance of Henry V,
before the Siege of Harfleur.

CHORUS
 Thus with imagined wing our swift scene flies
 In motion of no less celerity
 Than that of thought. Suppose that you have seen
 The well-appointed king at Dover pier
 Embark his royalty, and his brave fleet
 With silken streamers the young Phoebus fanning.
 Play with your fancies, and in them behold
 Upon the hempen tackle ship-boys climbing;
 Hear the shrill whistle, which doth order give
 To sounds confused; behold the threaden sails,
 Borne with th'invisible and creeping wind,
 Draw the huge bottoms through the furrowed sea,
 Breasting the lofty surge. O do but think
 You stand upon the rivage and behold
 A city on th'inconstant billows dancing—
 For so appears this fleet majestical,
 Holding due course to Harfleur. Follow, follow!
 Grapple your minds to sternage of this navy,
 And leave your England, as dead midnight still,
 Guarded with grandsires, babies, and old women,
 Either past or not arrived to pith and puissance.

For who is he, whose chin is but enriched
With one appearing hair, that will not follow
These culled and choice-drawn cavaliers to France?
Work, work your thoughts, and therein see a siege.
Behold the ordnance on their carriages,
With fatal mouths gaping on girded Harfleur.
Suppose th'ambassador from the French comes back,
Tells Harry that the King doth offer him
Catherine his daughter, and with her, to dowry,
Some petty and unprofitable dukedoms.
The offer likes not, and the nimble gunner
With linstock now the devilish cannon touches,
    Alarum, and chambers go off
And down goes all before them. Still be kind,
And eke out our performance with your mind.

             (*Henry V*, Prologue to Act Three)

Seeming

Hamlet, Prince of Denmark, speaks of his state of mind to his former fellow-students Rosencrantz and Guildenstern.

HAMLET ... I have of late—but wherefore I know not—lost all my mirth, forgone all custom of exercise; and indeed it goes so heavily with my disposition that this goodly frame, the earth, seems to me a sterile promontory. This most excellent canopy the air, look you, this brave o'erhanging, this majestical roof fretted with golden fire—why, it appears no other thing to me than a foul and pestilent congregation of vapours. What a piece of work is a man! How noble in reason, how infinite in faculty, in form and moving how express and admirable, in action how like an angel, in apprehension how like a god—the beauty of the world, the paragon of animals! And yet to me what is this quintessence of dust? Man delights not me—no, nor woman neither, though by your smiling you seem to say so.

(Hamlet, 2.2.296–311)

A Dream

Romeo speaks with his friend Mercutio.

ROMEO
    I dreamt a dream tonight.
MERCUTIO   And so did I.
ROMEO
    Well, what was yours?
MERCUTIO   That dreamers often lie.
ROMEO
    In bed asleep while they do dream things true.
MERCUTIO
    O, then I see Queen Mab hath been with you.
BENVOLIO   Queen Mab, what's she?
MERCUTIO
    She is the fairies' midwife, and she comes
    In shape no bigger than an agate stone
    On the forefinger of an alderman,
    Drawn with a team of little atomi
    Athwart men's noses as they lie asleep.
    Her wagon spokes made of long spinners' legs;
    The cover, of the wings of grasshoppers;
    Her traces, of the moonshine's wat'ry beams;
    Her collars, of the smallest spider web;
    Her whip, of cricket's bone, the lash of film;
    Her wagoner, a small grey-coated gnat
    Not half so big as a round little worm

Pricked from the lazy finger of a maid.
Her chariot is an empty hazelnut
Made by the joiner squirrel or old grub,
Time out o' mind the fairies' coachmakers.
And in this state she gallops night by night
Through lovers' brains, and then they dream of love;
O'er courtiers' knees, that dream on curtsies straight;
O'er ladies' lips, who straight on kisses dream,
Which oft the angry Mab with blisters plagues
Because their breaths with sweetmeats tainted are.
Sometime she gallops o'er a lawyer's lip,
And then dreams he of smelling out a suit;
And sometime comes she with a tithe-pig's tail
Tickling a parson's nose as a lies asleep;
Then dreams he of another benefice.
Sometime she driveth o'er a soldier's neck,
And then dreams he of cutting foreign throats,
Of breaches, ambuscados, Spanish blades,
Of healths five fathom deep; and then anon
Drums in his ear, at which he starts and wakes,
And being thus frighted, swears a prayer or two,
And sleeps again. This is that very Mab
That plaits the manes of horses in the night,
And bakes the elf-locks in foul sluttish hairs,
Which once untangled much misfortune bodes.
This is the hag, when maids lie on their backs,
That presses them and learns them first to bear,
Making them women of good carriage.
This is she—

ROMEO   Peace, peace, Mercutio, peace!
    Thou talk'st of nothing.
MERCUTIO   True. I talk of dreams,
    Which are the children of an idle brain,
    Begot of nothing but vain fantasy,
    Which is as thin of substance as the air,
    And more inconstant than the wind, who woos
    Even now the frozen bosom of the north,
    And, being angered, puffs away from thence,
    Turning his face to the dew-dropping south.
                              (*Romeo and Juliet*, 1.4.51–104)

The Power of Music

Prospero's spirit Ariel plays and sings to the shipwrecked Ferdinand.

> *Enter Ariel like a water-nymph, playing and singing,*
> *invisible to Ferdinand, who follows. Prospero and*
> *Miranda stand aside*

Song

ARIEL   Come unto these yellow sands,
        And then take hands;
     Curtsied when you have and kissed—
        The wild waves whist—
     Foot it featly here and there,
        And, sweet sprites, bear
     The burden. Hark, hark.

SPIRITS *(dispersedly within)*
        Bow-wow!

ARIEL   The watch-dogs bark.

SPIRITS *(within)* Bow-wow!

ARIEL   Hark, hark, I hear
     The strain of strutting Chanticleer
        Cry 'cock-a-diddle-dow'.

FERDINAND
     Where should this music be? I'th' air or th'earth?
     It sounds no more; and sure it waits upon
     Some god o'th' island. Sitting on a bank,

Weeping again the King my father's wreck,
This music crept by me upon the waters,
Allaying both their fury and my passion
With its sweet air. Thence I have followed it—
Or it hath drawn me rather. But 'tis gone.
No, it begins again.

Song

ARIEL   Full fathom five thy father lies.
                Of his bones are coral made;
            Those are pearls that were his eyes;
                Nothing of him that doth fade
            But doth suffer a sea-change
            Into something rich and strange.
                Sea-nymphs hourly ring his knell:
SPIRITS *(within)* Ding dong.
ARIEL   Hark, now I hear them.
SPIRITS *(within)*   Ding-dong bell.

FERDINAND
    The ditty does remember my drowned father.
    This is no mortal business, nor no sound
    That the earth owes.

                      (The Tempest, 1.2.378–411)

Sleep and Music

The monster Caliban speaks of the island where he lives.

CALIBAN Art thou afeard?
STEFANO No, monster, not I.
CALIBAN
>   Be not afeard. The isle is full of noises,
>   Sounds, and sweet airs, that give delight and hurt not.
>   Sometimes a thousand twangling instruments
>   Will hum about mine ears, and sometime voices
>   That if I then had waked after long sleep
>   Will make me sleep again; and then in dreaming
>   The clouds methought would open and show riches
>   Ready to drop upon me, that when I waked
>   I cried to dream again.

(The Tempest, 3.2.136–46)

Music and Love

At Belmont Lorenzo speaks with Jessica, with whom he has eloped.

LORENZO (*to Jessica*)
> . . . How sweet the moonlight sleeps upon this bank!
> Here will we sit, and let the sounds of music
> Creep in our ears. Soft stillness and the night
> Become the touches of sweet harmony.
> Sit, Jessica.
>> *They sit*
>>> Look how the floor of heaven
> Is thick inlaid with patens of bright gold.
> There's not the smallest orb which thou behold'st
> But in his motion like an angel sings,
> Still choiring to the young-eyed cherubins.
> Such harmony is in immortal souls,
> But whilst this muddy vesture of decay
> Doth grossly close it in, we cannot hear it.
>> *Enter Musicians*
> (*To the Musicians*) Come, ho, and wake Diana with a
>   hymn.
> With sweetest touches pierce your mistress' ear,
> And draw her home with music.
>> *The Musicians play*

JESSICA
> I am never merry when I hear sweet music.

LORENZO

    The reason is your spirits are attentive,
    For do but note a wild and wanton herd
    Or race of youthful and unhandled colts,
    Fetching mad bounds, bellowing and neighing loud,
    Which is the hot condition of their blood,
    If they but hear perchance a trumpet sound,
    Or any air of music touch their ears,
    You shall perceive them make a mutual stand,
    Their savage eyes turned to a modest gaze
    By the sweet power of music. Therefore the poet
    Did feign that Orpheus drew trees, stones, and floods,
    Since naught so stockish, hard, and full of rage
    But music for the time doth change his nature.
    The man that hath no music in himself,
    Nor is not moved with concord of sweet sounds,
    Is fit for treasons, stratagems, and spoils.
    The motions of his spirit are dull as night,
    And his affections dark as Erebus.
    Let no such man be trusted. Mark the music.

                   (The Merchant of Venice, 5.1.54–88)

Imagination's Tricks

Hippolyta and Duke Theseus have heard of the strange adventures of lovers in the Athenian woods.

HIPPOLYTA
    'Tis strange, my Theseus, that these lovers speak of.
THESEUS
    More strange than true. I never may believe
    These antique fables, nor these fairy toys.
    Lovers and madmen have such seething brains,
    Such shaping fantasies, that apprehend
    More than cool reason ever comprehends.
    The lunatic, the lover, and the poet
    Are of imagination all compact.
    One sees more devils than vast hell can hold:
    That is the madman. The lover, all as frantic,
    Sees Helen's beauty in a brow of Egypt.
    The poet's eye, in a fine frenzy rolling,
    Doth glance from heaven to earth, from earth to heaven,
    And as imagination bodies forth
    The forms of things unknown, the poet's pen
    Turns them to shapes, and gives to airy nothing
    A local habitation and a name.
    Such tricks hath strong imagination
    That if it would but apprehend some joy
    It comprehends some bringer of that joy;

Or in the night, imagining some fear,
How easy is a bush supposed a bear!

HIPPOLYTA

But all the story of the night told over,
And all their minds transfigured so together,
More witnesseth than fancy's images,
And grows to something of great constancy;
But howsoever, strange and admirable.

(A Midsummer Night's Dream, 5.1.1–27)

Consolation Rejected

John of Gaunt attempts to console his son Henry Bolingbroke, whom Richard II has exiled for six years.

JOHN OF GAUNT *(to Bolingbroke)*
>O, to what purpose dost thou hoard thy words,
>That thou return'st no greeting to thy friends?

BOLINGBROKE
>I have too few to take my leave of you,
>When the tongue's office should be prodigal
>To breathe the abundant dolour of the heart.

JOHN OF GAUNT
>Thy grief is but thy absence for a time.

BOLINGBROKE
>Joy absent, grief is present for that time.

JOHN OF GAUNT
>What is six winters? They are quickly gone.

BOLINGBROKE
>To men in joy, but grief makes one hour ten.

JOHN OF GAUNT
>Call it a travel that thou tak'st for pleasure.

BOLINGBROKE
>My heart will sigh when I miscall it so,
>Which finds it an enforcèd pilgrimage.

JOHN OF GAUNT
>The sullen passage of thy weary steps

Esteem as foil wherein thou art to set
The precious jewel of thy home return.

BOLINGBROKE

Nay, rather every tedious stride I make
Will but remember what a deal of world
I wander from the jewels that I love.
Must I not serve a long apprenticehood
To foreign passages, and in the end,
Having my freedom, boast of nothing else
But that I was a journeyman to grief?

JOHN OF GAUNT

All places that the eye of heaven visits
Are to a wise man ports and happy havens.
Teach thy necessity to reason thus:
There is no virtue like necessity.
Think not the King did banish thee,
But thou the King. Woe doth the heavier sit
Where it perceives it is but faintly borne.
Go, say I sent thee forth to purchase honour,
And not the King exiled thee; or suppose
Devouring pestilence hangs in our air
And thou art flying to a fresher clime.
Look what thy soul holds dear, imagine it
To lie that way thou goest, not whence thou com'st.
Suppose the singing birds musicians,
The grass whereon thou tread'st the presence
    strewed,
The flowers fair ladies, and thy steps no more
Than a delightful measure or a dance;

For gnarling sorrow hath less power to bite
The man that mocks at it and sets it light.

BOLINGBROKE

O, who can hold a fire in his hand
By thinking on the frosty Caucasus,
Or cloy the hungry edge of appetite
By bare imagination of a feast,
Or wallow naked in December snow
By thinking on fantastic summer's heat?
O no, the apprehension of the good
Gives but the greater feeling to the worse.
Fell sorrow's tooth doth never rankle more
Than when he bites, but lanceth not the sore.

(*Richard II*, original version: 1.3.242–66 with Additional Passage C)

The Insubstantial Pageant

The vision conjured up by Prospero's magic has vanished.

PROSPERO

> . . . Our revels now are ended. These our actors,
> As I foretold you, were all spirits, and
> Are melted into air, into thin air;
> And like the baseless fabric of this vision,
> The cloud-capped towers, the gorgeous palaces,
> The solemn temples, the great globe itself,
> Yea, all which it inherit, shall dissolve;
> And, like this insubstantial pageant faded,
> Leave not a rack behind. We are such stuff
> As dreams are made on, and our little life
> Is rounded with a sleep.

(The Tempest, 4.1.148–58)

Wisdom and Folly

Playing the Fool

Graziano tells Antonio of the part that he likes to play on the world's stage.

GRAZIANO   Let me play the fool.
   With mirth and laughter let old wrinkles come,
   And let my liver rather heat with wine
   Than my heart cool with mortifying groans.
   Why should a man whose blood is warm within
   Sit like his grandsire cut in alabaster,
   Sleep when he wakes, and creep into the jaundice
   By being peevish? I tell thee what, Antonio—
   I love thee, and 'tis my love that speaks—
   There are a sort of men whose visages
   Do cream and mantle like a standing pond,
   And do a wilful stillness entertain
   With purpose to be dressed in an opinion
   Of wisdom, gravity, profound conceit,
   As who should say 'I am Sir Oracle,
   And when I ope my lips, let no dog bark.'
   O my Antonio, I do know of these
   That therefore only are reputed wise
   For saying nothing, when I am very sure,
   If they should speak, would almost damn those ears
   Which, hearing them, would call their brothers fools.
                        (*The Merchant of Venice*, 1.1.79–99)

A Fool's Wisdom

Viola comments on the fool, Feste.

VIOLA

This fellow is wise enough to play the fool,
And to do that well craves a kind of wit.
He must observe their mood on whom he jests,
The quality of persons, and the time,
And, like the haggard, check at every feather
That comes before his eye. This is a practice
As full of labour as a wise man's art,
For folly that he wisely shows is fit,
But wise men, folly-fall'n, quite taint their wit.

(Twelfth Night, 3.1.59–67)

A Fool in the Forest

The courtier Jaques describes an encounter in the forest.

JAQUES

A fool, a fool, I met a fool i'th' forest,
A motley fool—a miserable world!—
As I do live by food, I met a fool,
Who laid him down and basked him in the sun,
And railed on Lady Fortune in good terms,
In good set terms, and yet a motley fool.
'Good morrow, fool,' quoth I. 'No, sir,' quoth he,
'Call me not fool till heaven hath sent me fortune.'
And then he drew a dial from his poke,
And looking on it with lack-lustre eye
Says very wisely 'It is ten o'clock.'
'Thus we may see', quoth he, 'how the world wags.
'Tis but an hour ago since it was nine,
And after one hour more 'twill be eleven.
And so from hour to hour we ripe and ripe,
And then from hour to hour we rot and rot;
And thereby hangs a tale.' When I did hear
The motley fool thus moral on the time
My lungs began to crow like chanticleer,
That fools should be so deep-contemplative,
And I did laugh sans intermission
An hour by his dial. O noble fool,
A worthy fool—motley's the only wear.

DUKE SENIOR What fool is this?

JAQUES

    O worthy fool!—One that hath been a courtier,
    And says 'If ladies be but young and fair
    They have the gift to know it.' And in his brain,
    Which is as dry as the remainder biscuit
    After a voyage, he hath strange places crammed
    With observation, the which he vents
    In mangled forms. O that I were a fool,
    I am ambitious for a motley coat.

DUKE SENIOR

    Thou shalt have one.

JAQUES   It is my only suit,
    Provided that you weed your better judgements
    Of all opinion that grows rank in them
    That I am wise. I must have liberty
    Withal, as large a charter as the wind,
    To blow on whom I please, for so fools have;
    And they that are most gallèd with my folly,
    They most must laugh. And why, sir, must they so?
    The why is plain as way to parish church:
    He that a fool doth very wisely hit
    Doth very foolishly, although he smart,
    Seem aught but senseless of the bob. If not,
    The wise man's folly is anatomized
    Even by the squandering glances of the fool.
    Invest me in my motley. Give me leave
    To speak my mind, and I will through and through

Cleanse the foul body of th'infected world,
If they will patiently receive my medicine.

(As You Like It, 2.7.12–61)

A Fool's Loyalty

King Lear's retinue has been reduced; his Fool comments.

FOOL

> . . . That sir which serves and seeks for gain
>   And follows but for form,
> Will pack when it begin to rain,
>   And leave thee in the storm.
>
> But I will tarry, the fool will stay,
>   And let the wise man fly.
> The knave turns fool that runs away,
>   The fool no knave, pardie.
>   *(The Tragedy of King Lear, 2.2.251–8)*

The Folly of Mourning

The Countess Olivia, mourning her brother's death, has given her professional fool Feste leave to prove that she is herself a fool.

FESTE Good madonna, why mournest thou?
OLIVIA Good fool, for my brother's death.
FESTE I think his soul is in hell, madonna.
OLIVIA I know his soul is in heaven, fool.
FESTE The more fool, madonna, to mourn for your brother's soul, being in heaven. Take away the fool, gentlemen.

(Twelfth Night, 1.5.62–8)

Intimations of Sobriety

Sir John Falstaff speaks of Prince Harry's brother, Prince John.

SIR JOHN . . . Good faith, this same young sober-blooded boy doth not love me, nor a man cannot make him laugh. But that's no marvel; he drinks no wine. There's never none of these demure boys come to any proof; for thin drink doth so overcool their blood, and making many fish meals, that they fall into a kind of male green-sickness; and then when they marry, they get wenches. They are generally fools and cowards—which some of us should be too, but for inflammation. A good sherry-sack hath a two-fold operation in it. It ascends me into the brain, dries me there all the foolish and dull and crudy vapours which environ it, makes it apprehensive, quick, forgetive, full of nimble, fiery, and delectable shapes, which, delivered o'er to the voice, the tongue, which is the birth, becomes excellent wit. The second property of your excellent sherry is the warming of the blood, which, before cold and settled, left the liver white and pale, which is the badge of pusillanimity and cowardice. But the sherry warms it, and makes it course from the inwards to the parts' extremes; it illuminateth the face, which, as a beacon, gives warning to all the rest of this little kingdom, man, to arm; and then the vital commoners and inland petty spirits muster me all to their captain, the heart; who, great and puffed up with his retinue, doth any deed of courage. And this valour comes of sherry. So that skill in the weapon is nothing without sack, for that sets it a-work; and learning a mere hoard of gold kept by a devil, till sack commences it and sets it in act and use. Hereof comes it that Prince Harry is valiant; for the cold blood he did naturally inherit of his father he hath, like lean, sterile, and bare land, manured, husbanded, and tilled, with excellent endeavour of drinking good, and good store of fertile sherry, that he is become very hot and valiant. If I had a thousand sons, the first human principle I would teach them should be to forswear thin potations, and to addict themselves to sack.

(*2 Henry IV*, 4.2.84–121)

Magic and Superstition

The Limits of Knowledge

Lafeu comments on Helen's apparently miraculous cure of the King.

LAFEU They say miracles are past, and we have our philo-
sophical persons to make modern and familiar things
supernatural and causeless. Hence is it that we make trifles
of terrors, ensconcing ourselves into seeming knowledge
when we should submit ourselves to an unknown fear.

(All's Well That Ends Well, 2.3.1–6)

Prodigies

Casca tells Cicero of the unnatural events on the eve of their planned assassination of Caesar.

CICERO

    Good even, Casca. Brought you Caesar home?
    Why are you breathless, and why stare you so?

CASCA

    Are not you moved, when all the sway of earth
    Shakes like a thing unfirm? O Cicero,
    I have seen tempests when the scolding winds
    Have rived the knotty oaks, and I have seen
    Th'ambitious ocean swell and rage and foam
    To be exalted with the threat'ning clouds;
    But never till tonight, never till now,
    Did I go through a tempest dropping fire.
    Either there is a civil strife in heaven,
    Or else the world, too saucy with the gods,
    Incenses them to send destruction.

CICERO

    Why, saw you anything more wonderful?

CASCA

    A common slave—you know him well by sight—
    Held up his left hand, which did flame and burn
    Like twenty torches joined; and yet his hand,
    Not sensible of fire, remained unscorched.

Besides—I ha' not since put up my sword—
Against the Capitol I met a lion
Who glazed upon me, and went surly by
Without annoying me. And there were drawn
Upon a heap a hundred ghastly women,
Transformèd with their fear, who swore they saw
Men all in fire walk up and down the streets.
And yesterday the bird of night did sit
Even at noonday upon the market-place,
Hooting and shrieking. When these prodigies
Do so conjointly meet, let not men say
'These are their reasons', 'they are natural',
For I believe they are portentous things
Unto the climate that they point upon.

CICERO
Indeed it is a strange-disposèd time;
But men may construe things after their fashion,
Clean from the purpose of the things themselves.

(*Julius Caesar*, 1.3.1–35)

Terrors of the Night

Macbeth is about to murder King Duncan.

MACBETH   . . . Now o'er the one half-world
    Nature seems dead, and wicked dreams abuse
    The curtained sleep. Witchcraft celebrates
    Pale Hecate's offerings, and withered murder,
    Alarumed by his sentinel the wolf,
    Whose howl's his watch, thus with his stealthy pace,
    With Tarquin's ravishing strides, towards his design
    Moves like a ghost. Thou sure and firm-set earth,
    Hear not my steps which way they walk, for fear
    Thy very stones prate of my whereabout,
    And take the present horror from the time,
    Which now suits with it.

(Macbeth, 2.1.49–60)

The Bird of Dawning

The ghost of Hamlet's father has 'faded on the crowing of the cock'.

MARCELLUS

    . . . Some say that ever 'gainst that season comes
Wherein our saviour's birth is celebrated
The bird of dawning singeth all night long;
And then, they say, no spirit can walk abroad,
The nights are wholesome; then no planets strike,
No fairy takes, nor witch hath power to charm,
So hallowed and so gracious is the time.

(Hamlet, 1.1.139–45)

The Fairies' Blessing

The newly married couples Theseus and Hippolyta, Lysander and Hermia, and Demetrius and Helena have retired to bed; it is 'fairy time'.

ROBIN

Now the hungry lion roars,
  And the wolf behowls the moon,
Whilst the heavy ploughman snores,
  All with weary task fordone.
Now the wasted brands do glow
  Whilst the screech-owl, screeching loud,
Puts the wretch that lies in woe
  In remembrance of a shroud.
Now it is the time of night
  That the graves, all gaping wide,
Every one lets forth his sprite
  In the churchway paths to glide;
And we fairies that do run
  By the triple Hecate's team
From the presence of the sun,
  Following darkness like a dream,
Now are frolic. Not a mouse
Shall disturb this hallowed house.
I am sent with broom before
To sweep the dust behind the door.

Enter Oberon and Titania, King and Queen of Fairies,
with all their train

OBERON

Through the house give glimmering light.
By the dead and drowsy fire
Every elf and fairy sprite
Hop as light as bird from brier,
And this ditty after me
Sing, and dance it trippingly.

TITANIA

First rehearse your song by rote,
To each word a warbling note.
Hand in hand with fairy grace
Will we sing and bless this place.

The song. The fairies dance

OBERON

Now until the break of day
Through this house each fairy stray.
To the best bride bed will we,
Which by us shall blessèd be,
And the issue there create
Ever shall be fortunate.
So shall all the couples three
Ever true in loving be,
And the blots of nature's hand
Shall not in their issue stand.
Never mole, harelip, nor scar,
Nor mark prodigious such as are

Despisèd in nativity
Shall upon their children be.
With this field-dew consecrate
Every fairy take his gait
And each several chamber bless
Through this palace with sweet peace;
And the owner of it blessed
Ever shall in safety rest.
Trip away, make no stay,
Meet me all by break of day.

(A Midsummer Night's Dream, 5.2.1–52)

A Fairy Lullaby

Titania, Queen of the Fairies, asks her attendants to sing her to sleep.

TITANIA

Come, now a roundel and a fairy song,
Then for the third part of a minute hence:
Some to kill cankers in the musk-rose buds,
Some war with reremice for their leathern wings
To make my small elves coats, and some keep back
The clamorous owl, that nightly hoots and wonders
At our quaint spirits. Sing me now asleep;
Then to your offices, and let me rest.
        She lies down. Fairies sing

FIRST FAIRY

You spotted snakes with double tongue,
    Thorny hedgehogs, be not seen;
Newts and blindworms, do no wrong;
    Come not near our Fairy Queen.

CHORUS (*dancing*)

Philomel with melody,
Sing in our sweet lullaby;
Lulla, lulla, lullaby; lulla, lulla, lullaby.
    Never harm
    Nor spell nor charm
Come our lovely lady nigh.
So good night, with lullaby.

FIRST FAIRY

> Weaving spiders, come not here;
>> Hence, you long-legged spinners, hence;
> Beetles black, approach not near;
>> Worm nor snail do no offence.

CHORUS (*dancing*)

> Philomel with melody,
> Sing in our sweet lullaby;
> Lulla, lulla, lullaby; lulla, lulla, lullaby.
>> Never harm
>> Nor spell nor charm
> Come our lovely lady nigh.
> So good night, with lullaby.
>> *Titania sleeps*

SECOND FAIRY

> Hence, away. Now all is well.
> One aloof stand sentinel.
>> (*A Midsummer Night's Dream*, 2.2.1–32)

Responsibility and Government

The Fable of the Honey Bees

*The Archbishop of Canterbury advises Henry V and his nobles that the
King may safely take some of his forces into France while leaving
others to defend England.*

EXETER

  . . . While that the armèd hand doth fight abroad,
  Th'advisèd head defends itself at home.
  For government, though high and low and lower,
  Put into parts, doth keep in one consent,
  Congreeing in a full and natural close,
  Like music.

CANTERBURY True. Therefore doth heaven divide
  The state of man in divers functions,
  Setting endeavour in continual motion;
  To which is fixèd, as an aim or butt,
  Obedience. For so work the honey-bees,
  Creatures that by a rule in nature teach
  The act of order to a peopled kingdom.
  They have a king, and officers of sorts,
  Where some like magistrates correct at home;
  Others like merchants venture trade abroad;
  Others like soldiers, armèd in their stings,
  Make boot upon the summer's velvet buds,
  Which pillage they with merry march bring home
  To the tent royal of their emperor,

Who busied in his majesty surveys
The singing masons building roofs of gold,
The civil citizens lading up the honey,
The poor mechanic porters crowding in
Their heavy burdens at his narrow gate,
The sad-eyed justice with his surly hum
Delivering o'er to executors pale
The lazy yawning drone. I this infer:
That many things, having full reference
To one consent, may work contrariously.
As many arrows, loosèd several ways,
Fly to one mark, as many ways meet in one town,
As many fresh streams meet in one salt sea,
As many lines close in the dial's centre,
So may a thousand actions once afoot
End in one purpose, and be all well borne
Without defect.

(Henry V, 1.2.178–213)

Degree

Ulysses urges that the Greeks must present a united front if they are to conquer Troy.

ULYSSES

    . . . When that the general is not like the hive
To whom the foragers shall all repair,
What honey is expected? Degree being vizarded,
Th'unworthiest shows as fairly in the masque
[   ]
The heavens themselves, the planets, and this centre
Observe degree, priority, and place,
Infixture, course, proportion, season, form,
Office and custom, in all line of order.
And therefore is the glorious planet Sol
In noble eminence enthroned and sphered
Amidst the other, whose med'cinable eye
Corrects the ill aspects of planets evil
And posts like the commandment of a king,
Sans check, to good and bad. But when the planets
In evil mixture to disorder wander,
What plagues and what portents, what mutiny?
What raging of the sea, shaking of earth?
Commotion in the winds, frights, changes, horrors
Divert and crack, rend and deracinate
The unity and married calm of states
Quite from their fixture. O when degree is shaked,

Which is the ladder to all high designs,
The enterprise is sick. How could communities,
Degrees in schools, and brotherhoods in cities,
Peaceful commerce from dividable shores,
The primogenity and due of birth,
Prerogative of age, crowns, sceptres, laurels,
But by degree stand in authentic place?
Take but degree away, untune that string,
And hark what discord follows. Each thing meets
In mere oppugnancy. The bounded waters
Should lift their bosoms higher than the shores
And make a sop of all this solid globe;
Strength should be lord of imbecility,
And the rude son should strike his father dead.
Force should be right—or rather, right and wrong,
Between whose endless jar justice resides,
Should lose their names, and so should justice too.
Then everything includes itself in power,
Power into will, will into appetite;
And appetite, an universal wolf,
So doubly seconded with will and power,
Must make perforce an universal prey,
And last eat up himself. Great Agamemnon,
This chaos, when degree is suffocate,
Follows the choking.
And this neglection of degree it is
That by a pace goes backward in a purpose
It hath to climb. The general's disdained
By him one step below; he, by the next;

That next, by him beneath. So every step,
Exampled by the first pace that is sick
Of his superior, grows to an envious fever
Of pale and bloodless emulation.
And 'tis this fever that keeps Troy on foot,
Not her own sinews. To end a tale of length:
Troy in our weakness lives, not in her strength.

(Troilus and Cressida, 1.3.80–137)

The Fable of the Belly

The patrician Menenius instructs Rome's rebellious citizens on their function in the commonwealth.

MENENIUS

There was a time when all the body's members,
Rebelled against the belly, thus accused it:
That only like a gulf it did remain
I'th' midst o'th' body, idle and unactive,
Still cupboarding the viand, never bearing
Like labour with the rest; where th'other instruments
Did see and hear, devise, instruct, walk, feel,
And, mutually participate, did minister
Unto the appetite and affection common
Of the whole body. The belly answered—

FIRST CITIZEN

Well, sir, what answer made the belly?

MENENIUS

Sir, I shall tell you. With a kind of smile,
Which ne'er came from the lungs, but even thus—
For look you, I may make the belly smile
As well as speak—it tauntingly replied
To th' discontented members, the mutinous parts
That envied his receipt; even so most fitly
As you malign our senators for that
They are not such as you.

FIRST CITIZEN   Your belly's answer—what?
    The kingly crownèd head, the vigilant eye,
    The counsellor heart, the arm our soldier,
    Our steed the leg, the tongue our trumpeter,
    With other muniments and petty helps
    In this our fabric, if that they—
MENENIUS   What then?
    Fore me, this fellow speaks! What then? What then?
FIRST CITIZEN
    Should by the cormorant belly be restrained,
    Who is the sink o'th' body—
MENENIUS   Well, what then?
FIRST CITIZEN
    The former agents, if they did complain,
    What could the belly answer?
MENENIUS   I will tell you,
    If you'll bestow a small of what you have little—
    Patience—a while, you'st hear the belly's answer.
FIRST CITIZEN
    You're long about it.
MENENIUS   Note me this, good friend:
    Your most grave belly was deliberate,
    Not rash like his accusers, and thus answered:
    'True is it, my incorporate friends,' quoth he,
    'That I receive the general food at first
    Which you do live upon, and fit it is,
    Because I am the storehouse and the shop
    Of the whole body. But, if you do remember,
    I send it through the rivers of your blood

Even to the court, the heart, to th' seat o'th' brain;
And through the cranks and offices of man
The strongest nerves and small inferior veins
From me receive that natural competency
Whereby they live. And though that all at once'—
You my good friends, this says the belly, mark me—

FIRST CITIZEN

Ay, sir, well, well.

MENENIUS   'Though all at once cannot
See what I do deliver out to each,
Yet I can make my audit up that all
From me do back receive the flour of all
And leave me but the bran.' What say you to't?

FIRST CITIZEN

It was an answer. How apply you this?

MENENIUS

The senators of Rome are this good belly,
And you the mutinous members. For examine
Their counsels and their cares, digest things rightly
Touching the weal o'th' common, you shall find
No public benefit which you receive
But it proceeds or comes from them to you,
And no way from yourselves.

(*Coriolanus*, 1.1.94–152)

A Dream of Sovereignty

The hunchback Richard of Gloucester expresses his ambitions.

RICHARD OF GLOUCESTER

    . . . Why, then, I do but dream on sovereignty
    Like one that stands upon a promontory
    And spies a far-off shore where he would tread,
    Wishing his foot were equal with his eye,
    And chides the sea that sunders him from thence,
    Saying he'll lade it dry to have his way—
    So do I wish the crown being so far off,
    And so I chide the means that keeps me from it,
    And so I say I'll cut the causes off,
    Flattering me with impossibilities.
    My eye's too quick, my heart o'erweens too much,
    Unless my hand and strength could equal them.
    Well, say there is no kingdom then for Richard—
    What other pleasure can the world afford?
    I'll make my heaven in a lady's lap,
    And deck my body in gay ornaments,
    And 'witch sweet ladies with my words and looks.
    O, miserable thought! And more unlikely
    Than to accomplish twenty golden crowns.
    Why, love forswore me in my mother's womb,
    And, for I should not deal in her soft laws,
    She did corrupt frail nature with some bribe

To shrink mine arm up like a withered shrub,
To make an envious mountain on my back—
Where sits deformity to mock my body—
To shape my legs of an unequal size,
To disproportion me in every part,
Like to a chaos, or an unlicked bear whelp
That carries no impression like the dam.
And am I then a man to be beloved?
O, monstrous fault, to harbour such a thought!
Then, since this earth affords no joy to me
But to command, to check, to o'erbear such
As are of better person than myself,
I'll make my heaven to dream upon the crown,
And whiles I live, t'account this world but hell,
Until my misshaped trunk that bears this head
Be round impalèd with a glorious crown.
And yet I know not how to get the crown,
For many lives stand between me and home.
And I—like one lost in a thorny wood,
That rends the thorns and is rent with the thorns,
Seeking a way and straying from the way,
Not knowing how to find the open air,
But toiling desperately to find it out—
Torment myself to catch the English crown.
And from that torment I will free myself,
Or hew my way out with a bloody axe.
Why, I can smile, and murder whiles I smile,
And cry 'Content!' to that which grieves my heart,
And wet my cheeks with artificial tears,

And frame my face to all occasions.
I'll drown more sailors than the mermaid shall;
I'll slay more gazers than the basilisk;
I'll play the orator as well as Nestor,
Deceive more slyly than Ulysses could,
And, like a Sinon, take another Troy.
I can add colours to the chameleon,
Change shapes with Proteus for advantages,
And set the murderous Machiavel to school.
Can I do this, and cannot get a crown?
Tut, were it farther off, I'll pluck it down.

(Richard, Duke of York (3 Henry VI), 3.2.134–95)

A King's Responsibilities

On the eve of the Battle of Agincourt, Henry V talks incognito to some of his soldiers.

> *Enter three soldiers: John Bates, Alexander Court, and Michael Williams*

COURT Brother John Bates, is not that the morning which breaks yonder?

BATES I think it be. But we have no great cause to desire the approach of day.

WILLIAMS We see yonder the beginning of the day, but I think we shall never see the end of it.—Who goes there?

KING HARRY (*disguised*) A friend.

WILLIAMS Under what captain serve you?

KING HARRY Under Sir Thomas Erpingham.

WILLIAMS A good old commander and a most kind gentleman. I pray you, what thinks he of our estate?

KING HARRY Even as men wrecked upon a sand, that look to be washed off the next tide.

BATES He hath not told his thought to the King?

KING HARRY No, nor it is not meet he should. For though I speak it to you, I think the King is but a man, as I am. The violet smells to him as it doth to me; the element shows to him as it doth to me. All his senses have but human conditions. His ceremonies laid by, in his nakedness he appears but a man, and though his affections are higher mounted than ours, yet when they stoop, they stoop with the like wing. Therefore, when he sees reason of fears, as we do, his fears, out of doubt, be of the same relish as ours are. Yet, in reason, no man should possess him with any appearance of fear, lest he, by showing it, should dishearten his army.

BATES He may show what outward courage he will, but I believe, as cold a night as 'tis, he could wish himself in Thames up to the neck. And so I would he were, and I by him, at all adventures, so we were quit here.

KING HARRY By my troth, I will speak my conscience of the King. I think he would not wish himself anywhere but where he is.

BATES Then I would he were here alone. So should he be sure to be ransomed, and a many poor men's lives saved.

KING HARRY I dare say you love him not so ill to wish him here alone, howsoever you speak this to feel other men's minds. Methinks I could not die anywhere so contented as in the King's company, his cause being just and his quarrel honourable.

WILLIAMS That's more than we know.

BATES Ay, or more than we should seek after. For we know enough if we know we are the King's subjects. If his cause be wrong, our obedience to the King wipes the crime of it out of us.

WILLIAMS But if the cause be not good, the King himself hath a heavy reckoning to make, when all those legs and arms and heads chopped off in a battle shall join together at the latter day, and cry all, 'We died at such a place'—some swearing, some crying for a surgeon, some upon their wives left poor behind them, some upon the debts they owe, some upon their children rawly left. I am afeard there are few die well that die in a battle, for how can they charitably dispose of anything, when blood is their argument? Now, if these men do not die well, it will be a black matter for the King that led them to it—who to disobey were against all proportion of subjection.

KING HARRY So, if a son that is by his father sent about merchandise do sinfully miscarry upon the sea, the imputation of his wickedness, by your rule, should be imposed upon his father, that sent him. Or if a servant, under his master's command transporting a sum of money, be assailed by robbers, and die in many irreconciled iniquities, you may call the business of the master the author of the servant's damnation. But this is not so. The King is not bound to answer the particular endings of his soldiers, the father of his son, nor the master of his servant, for they purpose not their deaths when they propose their services. Besides, there is no king, be his cause never so spotless, if it come to the arbitrament of swords, can try it out with all unspotted soldiers. Some, peradventure, have on them the guilt of premeditated and contrived murder; some, of beguiling virgins with the broken seals of perjury; some, making the wars their bulwark, that have before gored the gentle bosom of peace with pillage and robbery. Now, if these men have defeated the law and outrun native punishment, though they can outstrip men, they have no wings to fly from God. War is his beadle. War is his vengeance. So that here men are punished for before-breach of the King's laws, in now the King's quarrel. Where they feared the death, they have borne life away; and where they would be safe, they perish. Then if they die unprovided, no more is the King guilty of their damnation than he was before guilty of those impieties for the which they are now visited. Every subject's duty is the King's, but every subject's soul is his own. Therefore should every soldier in the wars do as every sick man in his bed: wash every mote out of his conscience. And dying so, death is to him advantage; or not dying, the time was blessedly lost wherein such preparation was gained. And in him that escapes, it were not sin to think that, making God so free an offer, he let him outlive that day to see his greatness and to teach others how they should prepare.

BATES 'Tis certain, every man that dies ill, the ill upon his own head. The King is not to answer it. I do not desire he should answer for me, and yet I determine to fight lustily for him.

(Henry V, 4.1.85–188)

A Leader's Speech

Henry V stirs up his army during the Siege of Harfleur.

KING HARRY

Once more unto the breach, dear friends, once more,
Or close the wall up with our English dead.
In peace there's nothing so becomes a man
As modest stillness and humility,
But when the blast of war blows in our ears,
Then imitate the action of the tiger.
Stiffen the sinews, conjure up the blood,
Disguise fair nature with hard-favoured rage.
Then lend the eye a terrible aspect,
Let it pry through the portage of the head
Like the brass cannon, let the brow o'erwhelm it
As fearfully as doth a gallèd rock
O'erhang and jutty his confounded base,
Swilled with the wild and wasteful ocean.
Now set the teeth and stretch the nostril wide,
Hold hard the breath, and bend up every spirit
To his full height. On, on, you noblest English,
Whose blood is fet from fathers of war-proof,
Fathers that like so many Alexanders
Have in these parts from morn till even fought,
And sheathed their swords for lack of argument.
Dishonour not your mothers; now attest

That those whom you called fathers did beget you.
Be copy now to men of grosser blood,
And teach them how to war. And you, good yeomen,
Whose limbs were made in England, show us here
The mettle of your pasture; let us swear
That you are worth your breeding—which I doubt not,
For there is none of you so mean and base
That hath not noble lustre in your eyes.
I see you stand like greyhounds in the slips,
Straining upon the start. The game's afoot.
Follow your spirit, and upon this charge
Cry, 'God for Harry! England and Saint George!'

(Henry V, 3.1)

The Glory of Honour

Henry V speaks to his fellow-soldiers before the Battle of Agincourt.

WARWICK   O that we now had here
But one ten thousand of those men in England
That do no work today.

KING HARRY   What's he that wishes so?
My cousin Warwick? No, my fair cousin.
If we are marked to die, we are enough
To do our country loss; and if to live,
The fewer men, the greater share of honour.
God's will, I pray thee wish not one man more.
By Jove, I am not covetous for gold,
Nor care I who doth feed upon my cost;
It ernes me not if men my garments wear;
Such outward things dwell not in my desires.
But if it be a sin to covet honour
I am the most offending soul alive.
No, faith, my coz, wish not a man from England.
God's peace, I would not lose so great an honour
As one man more methinks would share from me
For the best hope I have. O do not wish one more.
Rather proclaim it presently through my host
That he which hath no stomach to this fight,
Let him depart. His passport shall be made

And crowns for convoy put into his purse.
We would not die in that man's company
That fears his fellowship to die with us.
This day is called the Feast of Crispian.
He that outlives this day and comes safe home
Will stand a-tiptoe when this day is named
And rouse him at the name of Crispian.
He that shall see this day and live t'old age
Will yearly on the vigil feast his neighbours
And say, 'Tomorrow is Saint Crispian.'
Then will he strip his sleeve and show his scars
And say, 'These wounds I had on Crispin's day.'
Old men forget; yet all shall be forgot,
But he'll remember, with advantages,
What feats he did that day. Then shall our names,
Familiar in his mouth as household words—
Harry the King, Bedford and Exeter,
Warwick and Talbot, Salisbury and Gloucester—
Be in their flowing cups freshly remembered.
This story shall the good man teach his son,
And Crispin Crispian shall ne'er go by
From this day to the ending of the world
But we in it shall be rememberèd,
We few, we happy few, we band of brothers.
For he today that sheds his blood with me
Shall be my brother; be he ne'er so vile,
This day shall gentle his condition.
And gentlemen in England now abed
Shall think themselves accursed they were not here,

And hold their manhoods cheap whiles any speaks
That fought with us upon Saint Crispin's day.

(Henry V, 4.3.16–67)

Leadership

The Chorus addresses the audience before the Battle of Agincourt.

CHORUS

    Now entertain conjecture of a time
    When creeping murmur and the poring dark
    Fills the wide vessel of the universe.
    From camp to camp through the foul womb of night
    The hum of either army stilly sounds,
    That the fixed sentinels almost receive
    The secret whispers of each other's watch.
    Fire answers fire, and through their paly flames
    Each battle sees the other's umbered face.
    Steed threatens steed, in high and boastful neighs
    Piercing the night's dull ear, and from the tents
    The armourers, accomplishing the knights,
    With busy hammers closing rivets up,
    Give dreadful note of preparation.
    The country cocks do crow, the clocks do toll
    And the third hour of drowsy morning name.
    Proud of their numbers and secure in soul,
    The confident and overlusty French
    Do the low-rated English play at dice,
    And chide the cripple tardy-gaited night,
    Who like a foul and ugly witch doth limp
    So tediously away. The poor condemnèd English,

Like sacrifices, by their watchful fires
Sit patiently and inly ruminate
The morning's danger; and their gesture sad,
Investing lank lean cheeks and war-worn coats,
Presented them unto the gazing moon
So many horrid ghosts. O now, who will behold
The royal captain of this ruined band
Walking from watch to watch, from tent to tent,
Let him cry, 'Praise and glory on his head!'
For forth he goes and visits all his host,
Bids them good morrow with a modest smile
And calls them brothers, friends, and countrymen.
Upon his royal face there is no note
How dread an army hath enrounded him;
Nor doth he dedicate one jot of colour
Unto the weary and all-watchèd night,
But freshly looks and overbears attaint
With cheerful semblance and sweet majesty,
That every wretch, pining and pale before,
Beholding him, plucks comfort from his looks.
A largess universal, like the sun,
His liberal eye doth give to everyone,
Thawing cold fear, that mean and gentle all
Behold, as may unworthiness define,
A little touch of Harry in the night.
And so our scene must to the battle fly,
Where O for pity, we shall much disgrace,
With four or five most vile and ragged foils,
Right ill-disposed in brawl ridiculous,

The name of Agincourt. Yet sit and see,
Minding true things by what their mock'ries be.

(Henry V, Prologue to Act Four)

Self-command

They that have power to hurt and will do none,
That do not do the thing they most do show,
Who moving others are themselves as stone,
Unmovèd, cold, and to temptation slow—
They rightly do inherit heaven's graces,
And husband nature's riches from expense;
They are the lords and owners of their faces,
Others but stewards of their excellence.
The summer's flower is to the summer sweet
Though to itself it only live and die,
But if that flower with base infection meet
The basest weed outbraves his dignity;
   For sweetest things turn sourest by their deeds:
   Lilies that fester smell far worse than weeds.

(Sonnet 94)

Mercy

Shylock has asked how he can be compelled to show mercy to his victim.

PORTIA
> The quality of mercy is not strained.
> It droppeth as the gentle rain from heaven
> Upon the place beneath. It is twice blest:
> It blesseth him that gives, and him that takes.
> 'Tis mightiest in the mightiest. It becomes
> The thronèd monarch better than his crown.
> His sceptre shows the force of temporal power,
> The attribute to awe and majesty,
> Wherein doth sit the dread and fear of kings;
> But mercy is above this sceptred sway.
> It is enthronèd in the hearts of kings;
> It is an attribute to God himself,
> And earthly power doth then show likest God's
> When mercy seasons justice.

> > *(The Merchant of Venice, 4.1.181–94)*

Outward Fame

As the Duke of Clarence sleeps, fearful of his life, his keeper meditates.

BRACKENBURY

> . . . Sorrow breaks seasons and reposing hours,
> Makes the night morning and the noontide night.
> Princes have but their titles for their glories,
> An outward honour for an inward toil,
> And for unfelt imaginations
> They often feel a world of restless cares;
> So that, between their titles and low name,
> There's nothing differs but the outward fame.

> *(Richard III, 1.4.72–9)*

Ceremony

King Henry V's soldiers have suggested (see pp. 240–3) that he is
personally responsible for them, body and soul.

KING HARRY

   . . . Upon the King.

'Let us our lives, our souls, our debts, our care-full
  wives,

Our children, and our sins, lay on the King.'

We must bear all. O hard condition,

Twin-born with greatness: subject to the breath

Of every fool, whose sense no more can feel

But his own wringing. What infinite heartsease

Must kings neglect that private men enjoy?

And what have kings that privates have not too,

Save ceremony, save general ceremony?

And what art thou, thou idol ceremony?

What kind of god art thou, that suffer'st more

Of mortal griefs than do thy worshippers?

What are thy rents? What are thy comings-in?

O ceremony, show me but thy worth.

What is thy soul of adoration?

Art thou aught else but place, degree, and form,

Creating awe and fear in other men?

Wherein thou art less happy, being feared,

Than they in fearing.

What drink'st thou oft, instead of homage sweet,
But poisoned flattery? O be sick, great greatness,
And bid thy ceremony give thee cure.
Think'st thou the fiery fever will go out
With titles blown from adulation?
Will it give place to flexure and low bending?
Canst thou, when thou command'st the beggar's knee,
Command the health of it? No, thou proud dream
That play'st so subtly with a king's repose;
I am a king that find thee, and I know
'Tis not the balm, the sceptre, and the ball,
The sword, the mace, the crown imperial,
The intertissued robe of gold and pearl,
The farcèd title running fore the king,
The throne he sits on, nor the tide of pomp
That beats upon the high shore of this world—
No, not all these, thrice-gorgeous ceremony,
Not all these, laid in bed majestical,
Can sleep so soundly as the wretched slave
Who with a body filled and vacant mind
Gets him to rest, crammed with distressful bread;
Never sees horrid night, the child of hell,
But like a lackey from the rise to set
Sweats in the eye of Phoebus, and all night
Sleeps in Elysium; next day, after dawn
Doth rise and help Hyperion to his horse,
And follows so the ever-running year
With profitable labour to his grave.
And but for ceremony such a wretch,

Winding up days with toil and nights with sleep,
Had the forehand and vantage of a king.
The slave, a member of the country's peace,
Enjoys it, but in gross brain little wots
What watch the King keeps to maintain the peace,
Whose hours the peasant best advantages.

(Henry V, 4.1.227–81)

Responsibility Abused

Exercising his power as deputy for the Duke of Vienna, Angelo has sentenced Isabella's brother Claudio to death for fornication.

ISABELLA Could great men thunder
    As Jove himself does, Jove would never be quiet,
    For every pelting petty officer
    Would use his heaven for thunder, nothing but thunder.
    Merciful heaven,
    Thou rather with thy sharp and sulphurous bolt
    Split'st the unwedgeable and gnarlèd oak
    Than the soft myrtle. But man, proud man,
    Dressed in a little brief authority,
    Most ignorant of what he's most assured,
    His glassy essence, like an angry ape
    Plays such fantastic tricks before high heaven
    As makes the angels weep, who, with our spleens,
    Would all themselves laugh mortal.

(Measure for Measure, 2.2.113–26)

A King Envies a Shepherd

*The weak King Henry VI has been sent off the battlefield by his queen
and her allies.*

KING HENRY

 This battle fares like to the morning's war,
  When dying clouds contend with growing light,
 What time the shepherd, blowing of his nails,
  Can neither call it perfect day nor night.
 Now sways it this way like a mighty sea
  Forced by the tide to combat with the wind,
 Now sways it that way like the selfsame sea
  Forced to retire by fury of the wind.
 Sometime the flood prevails, and then the wind;
 Now one the better, then another best—
 Both tugging to be victors, breast to breast,
 Yet neither conqueror nor conquerèd.
 So is the equal poise of this fell war.
 Here on this molehill will I sit me down.
 To whom God will, there be the victory.
 For Margaret my queen, and Clifford, too,
 Have chid me from the battle, swearing both
 They prosper best of all when I am thence.
 Would I were dead, if God's good will were so—
 For what is in this world but grief and woe?
 O God! Methinks it were a happy life

To be no better than a homely swain.
To sit upon a hill, as I do now;
To carve out dials quaintly, point by point,
Thereby to see the minutes how they run:
How many makes the hour full complete,
How many hours brings about the day,
How many days will finish up the year,
How many years a mortal man may live.
When this is known, then to divide the times:
So many hours must I tend my flock,
So many hours must I take my rest,
So many hours must I contemplate,
So many hours must I sport myself,
So many days my ewes have been with young,
So many weeks ere the poor fools will ean,
So many years ere I shall shear the fleece.
So minutes, hours, days, weeks, months, and years,
Passed over to the end they were created,
Would bring white hairs unto a quiet grave.
Ah, what a life were this! How sweet! How lovely!
Gives not the hawthorn bush a sweeter shade
To shepherds looking on their seely sheep
Than doth a rich embroidered canopy
To kings that fear their subjects' treachery?
O yes, it doth—a thousandfold it doth.
And to conclude, the shepherd's homely curds,
His cold thin drink out of his leather bottle,
His wonted sleep under a fresh tree's shade,
All which secure and sweetly he enjoys,

Is far beyond a prince's delicates,
His viands sparkling in a golden cup,
His body couchèd in a curious bed,
When care, mistrust, and treason waits on him.
(Richard, Duke of York (3 Henry VI), 2.5.1–54)

The Head that Wears a Crown

Cares of state prevent King Henry IV from sleeping.

KING HENRY

    . . . How many thousand of my poorest subjects
Are at this hour asleep? O sleep, O gentle sleep,
Nature's soft nurse, how have I frighted thee,
That thou no more wilt weigh my eyelids down
And steep my senses in forgetfulness?
Why rather, sleep, liest thou in smoky cribs,
Upon uneasy pallets stretching thee,
And hushed with buzzing night-flies to thy slumber,
Than in the perfumed chambers of the great,
Under the canopies of costly state,
And lulled with sound of sweetest melody?
O thou dull god, why li'st thou with the vile
In loathsome beds, and leav'st the kingly couch
A watch-case, or a common 'larum-bell?
Wilt thou upon the high and giddy mast
Seal up the ship-boy's eyes, and rock his brains
In cradle of the rude imperious surge,
And in the visitation of the winds,
Who take the ruffian billows by the top,
Curling their monstrous heads, and hanging them
With deafing clamour in the slippery clouds,
That, with the hurly, death itself awakes?

Canst thou, O partial sleep, give thy repose
To the wet sea-boy in an hour so rude,
And in the calmest and most stillest night,
With all appliances and means to boot,
Deny it to a king? Then happy low, lie down.
Uneasy lies the head that wears a crown.

(*2 Henry IV*, 3.1.4–31)

Renunciation (1)

At Flint Castle Richard II begins to yield to the usurping Henry Bolingbroke.

KING RICHARD

What must the King do now? Must he submit?
The King shall do it. Must he be deposed?
The King shall be contented. Must he lose
The name of King? A God's name, let it go.
I'll give my jewels for a set of beads,
My gorgeous palace for a hermitage,
My gay apparel for an almsman's gown,
My figured goblets for a dish of wood,
My sceptre for a palmer's walking staff,
My subjects for a pair of carvèd saints,
And my large kingdom for a little grave,
A little, little grave, an obscure grave;
Or I'll be buried in the King's highway,
Some way of common trade where subjects' feet
May hourly trample on their sovereign's head,
For on my heart they tread now, whilst I live,
And buried once, why not upon my head?
Aumerle, thou weep'st, my tender-hearted cousin.
We'll make foul weather with despisèd tears.
Our sighs and they shall lodge the summer corn,
And make a dearth in this revolting land.

Or shall we play the wantons with our woes,
And make some pretty match with shedding tears;
As thus to drop them still upon one place
Till they have fretted us a pair of graves
Within the earth, and therein laid? 'There lies
Two kinsmen digged their graves with weeping eyes.'
Would not this ill do well? Well, well, I see
I talk but idly and you mock at me.
Most mighty prince, my lord Northumberland,
What says King Bolingbroke? Will his majesty
Give Richard leave to live till Richard die?
You make a leg, and Bolingbroke says 'Ay'.

NORTHUMBERLAND

My lord, in the base court he doth attend
To speak with you. May it please you to come down?

KING RICHARD

Down, down I come like glist'ring Phaëton,
Wanting the manage of unruly jades.
In the base court: base court where kings grow base
To come at traitors' calls, and do them grace.
In the base court, come down: down court, down King,
For night-owls shriek where mounting larks should sing.

(Richard II, 3.3.142–82)

Renunciation (2)

Richard II resigns his crown to the usurper Henry Bolingbroke, later Henry IV.

BOLINGBROKE

> I thought you had been willing to resign.

RICHARD

> My crown I am, but still my griefs are mine.
> You may my glories and my state depose,
> But not my griefs; still am I king of those.

BOLINGBROKE

> Part of your cares you give me with your crown.

RICHARD

> Your cares set up do not pluck my cares down.
> My care is loss of care by old care done;
> Your care is gain of care by new care won.
> The cares I give I have, though given away;
> They 'tend the crown, yet still with me they stay.

BOLINGBROKE

> Are you contented to resign the crown?

RICHARD

> Ay, no; no, ay; for I must nothing be;
> Therefore no, no, for I resign to thee.
> Now mark me how I will undo myself.
> I give this heavy weight from off my head,
>> *Bolingbroke accepts the crown*

And this unwieldy sceptre from my hand,
> *Bolingbroke accepts the sceptre*

The pride of kingly sway from out my heart.
With mine own tears I wash away my balm,
With mine own hands I give away my crown,
With mine own tongue deny my sacred state,
With mine own breath release all duteous oaths.
All pomp and majesty I do forswear.
My manors, rents, revenues I forgo.
My acts, decrees, and statutes I deny.
God pardon all oaths that are broke to me.
God keep all vows unbroke are made to thee.
Make me, that nothing have, with nothing grieved,
And thou with all pleased, that hast all achieved.
Long mayst thou live in Richard's seat to sit,
And soon lie Richard in an earthy pit.
'God save King Henry,' unkinged Richard says,
'And send him many years of sunshine days.'

(Richard II, 4.1.180–211)

Supernatural Power Renounced

Though Prospero's enemies are in his power, he has decided that 'The rarer action is | In virtue than in vengeance'.

PROSPERO

Ye elves of hills, brooks, standing lakes and groves,
And ye that on the sands with printless foot
Do chase the ebbing Neptune, and do fly him
When he comes back; you demi-puppets that
By moonshine do the green sour ringlets make
Whereof the ewe not bites; and you whose pastime
Is to make midnight mushrooms, that rejoice
To hear the solemn curfew; by whose aid,
Weak masters though ye be, I have bedimmed
The noontide sun, called forth the mutinous winds,
And 'twixt the green sea and the azured vault
Set roaring war—to the dread rattling thunder
Have I given fire, and rifted Jove's stout oak
With his own bolt; the strong-based promontory
Have I made shake, and by the spurs plucked up
The pine and cedar; graves at my command
Have waked their sleepers, oped, and let 'em forth
By my so potent art. But this rough magic
I here abjure. And when I have required
Some heavenly music—which even now I do—
To work mine end upon their senses that

This airy charm is for, I'll break my staff,
Bury it certain fathoms in the earth,
And deeper than did ever plummet sound
I'll drown my book.

(The Tempest, 5.1.33–57)

Time

A Spring Song

It was a lover and his lass,
  With a hey, and a ho, and a hey-nonny-no,
That o'er the green cornfield did pass
  In spring-time, the only pretty ring-time,
When birds do sing, hey ding-a-ding ding,
Sweet lovers love the spring.

Between the acres of the rye,
  With a hey, and a ho, and a hey-nonny-no,
These pretty country folks would lie,
  In spring-time, the only pretty ring-time,
When birds do sing, hey ding-a-ding ding,
Sweet lovers love the spring.

This carol they began that hour,
  With a hey, and a ho, and a hey-nonny-no,
How that a life was but a flower,
  In spring-time, the only pretty ring-time,
When birds do sing, hey ding-a-ding ding,
Sweet lovers love the spring.

And therefore take the present time,
  With a hey, and a ho, and a hey-nonny-no,
For love is crownèd with the prime,
  In spring time, the only pretty ring-time,

When birds do sing, hey ding-a-ding,
Sweet lovers love the spring.
(As You Like It, 5.3.15–38)

Relativity

In the Forest of Ardenne Rosalind, disguised as Ganymede, talks with her lover, Orlando.

ROSALIND I pray you, what is't o'clock?

ORLANDO You should ask me what time o' day. There's no clock in the forest.

ROSALIND Then there is no true lover in the forest, else sighing every minute and groaning every hour would detect the lazy foot of time as well as a clock.

ORLANDO And why not the swift foot of time? Had not that been as proper?

ROSALIND By no means, sir. Time travels in divers paces with divers persons. I'll tell you who time ambles withal, who time trots withal, who time gallops withal, and who he stands still withal.

ORLANDO I prithee, who doth he trot withal?

ROSALIND Marry, he trots hard with a young maid between the contract of her marriage and the day it is solemnized. If the interim be but a se'nnight, time's pace is so hard that it seems the length of seven year.

ORLANDO Who ambles time withal?

ROSALIND With a priest that lacks Latin, and a rich man that hath not the gout; for the one sleeps easily because he cannot study, and the other lives merrily because he feels no pain, the one lacking the burden of lean and wasteful learning, the other knowing no burden of heavy tedious penury. These time ambles withal.

ORLANDO Who doth he gallop withal?

ROSALIND With a thief to the gallows; for though he go as softly as foot can fall, he thinks himself too soon there.

ORLANDO Who stays it still withal?

ROSALIND With lawyers in the vacation; for they sleep between term and term, and then they perceive not how time moves.

(As You Like It, 3.2.293–324)

A Defence against Time

When I do count the clock that tells the time,
And see the brave day sunk in hideous night;
When I behold the violet past prime,
And sable curls ensilvered o'er with white;
When lofty trees I see barren of leaves,
Which erst from heat did canopy the herd,
And summer's green all girded up in sheaves
Borne on the bier with white and bristly beard:
Then of thy beauty do I question make
That thou among the wastes of time must go,
Since sweets and beauties do themselves forsake,
And die as fast as they see others grow;
　And nothing 'gainst time's scythe can make defence
　Save breed to brave him when he takes thee hence.

(Sonnet 12)

Poetic Immortality

Not marble nor the gilded monuments
Of princes shall outlive this powerful rhyme,
But you shall shine more bright in these contents
Than unswept stone besmeared with sluttish time.
When wasteful war shall statues overturn,
And broils root out the work of masonry,
Nor Mars his sword nor war's quick fire shall burn
The living record of your memory.
'Gainst death and all oblivious enmity
Shall you pace forth; your praise shall still find room
Even in the eyes of all posterity
That wear this world out to the ending doom.
  So, till the judgement that yourself arise,
  You live in this, and dwell in lovers' eyes.

(Sonnet 55)

Time Defied

Like as the waves make towards the pebbled shore,
So do our minutes hasten to their end,
Each changing place with that which goes before;
In sequent toil all forwards do contend.
Nativity, once in the main of light,
Crawls to maturity, wherewith being crowned
Crookèd eclipses 'gainst his glory fight,
And time that gave doth now his gift confound.
Time doth transfix the flourish set on youth,
And delves the parallels in beauty's brow;
Feeds on the rarities of nature's truth,
And nothing stands but for his scythe to mow.
   And yet to times in hope my verse shall stand,
   Praising thy worth despite his cruel hand.

(Sonnet 60)

Love's Illusion

To me, fair friend, you never can be old;
For as you were when first your eye I eyed,
Such seems your beauty still. Three winters cold
Have from the forests shook three summers' pride;
Three beauteous springs to yellow autumn turned
In process of the seasons have I seen,
Three April perfumes in three hot Junes burned
Since first I saw you fresh, which yet are green.
Ah yet doth beauty, like a dial hand,
Steal from his figure and no pace perceived;
So your sweet hue, which methinks still doth stand,
Hath motion, and mine eye may be deceived.
  For fear of which, hear this, thou age unbred:
  Ere you were born was beauty's summer dead.

(Sonnet 104)

The Poet's Fight against Time

Since brass, nor stone, nor earth, nor boundless sea,
But sad mortality o'ersways their power,
How with this rage shall beauty hold a plea,
Whose action is no stronger than a flower?
O how shall summer's honey breath hold out
Against the wrackful siege of battering days
When rocks impregnable are not so stout,
Nor gates of steel so strong, but time decays?
O fearful meditation! Where, alack,
Shall time's best jewel from time's chest lie hid,
Or what strong hand can hold his swift foot back,
Or who his spoil of beauty can forbid?
  O none, unless this miracle have might:
  That in black ink my love may still shine bright.

(Sonnet 65)

Time's Glory

The raped Lucrece meditates.

Time's glory is to calm contending kings,
To unmask falsehood and bring truth to light,
To stamp the seal of time in agèd things,
To wake the morn and sentinel the night,
To wrong the wronger till he render right,
  To ruinate proud buildings with thy hours
  And smear with dust their glitt'ring golden towers;

To fill with worm-holes stately monuments,
To feed oblivion with decay of things,
To blot old books and alter their contents,
To pluck the quills from ancient ravens' wings,
To dry the old oak's sap and blemish springs,
  To spoil antiquities of hammered steel,
  And turn the giddy round of fortune's wheel;

To show the beldame daughters of her daughter,
To make the child a man, the man a child,
To slay the tiger that doth live by slaughter,
To tame the unicorn and lion wild,
To mock the subtle in themselves beguiled,
  To cheer the ploughman with increaseful crops,
  And waste huge stones with little water drops.

(The Rape of Lucrece, 939–59)

Envious Time

The once-great Grecian warrior Achilles has ceased to exert himself.
Ulysses warns him that reputation must continually be renewed.

ULYSSES   Time hath, my lord,
  A wallet at his back, wherein he puts
  Alms for oblivion, a great-sized monster
  Of ingratitudes. Those scraps are good deeds past,
  Which are devoured as fast as they are made,
  Forgot as soon as done. Perseverance, dear my lord,
  Keeps honour bright. To have done is to hang
  Quite out of fashion, like a rusty mail
  In monumental mock'ry. Take the instant way,
  For honour travels in a strait so narrow,
  Where one but goes abreast. Keep then the path,
  For emulation hath a thousand sons
  That one by one pursue: if you give way,
  Or hedge aside from the direct forthright,
  Like to an entered tide they all rush by
  And leave you hindmost;
  Or, like a gallant horse fall'n in first rank,
  Lie there for pavement to the abject rear,
  O'errun and trampled on. Then what they do in present,
  Though less than yours in past, must o'ertop yours.
  For Time is like a fashionable host,
  That slightly shakes his parting guest by th' hand

And, with his arms outstretched as he would fly,
Grasps in the comer. Welcome ever smiles,
And Farewell goes out sighing. O let not virtue seek
Remuneration for the thing it was;
For beauty, wit,
High birth, vigour of bone, desert in service,
Love, friendship, charity, are subjects all
To envious and calumniating time.
One touch of nature makes the whole world kin—
That all with one consent praise new-born gauds,
Though they are made and moulded of things past,
And give to dust that is a little gilt
More laud than gilt o'er-dusted.
The present eye praises the present object.

(Troilus and Cressida, 3.3.139–74)

The Chimes at Midnight

*After many years Sir John Falstaff has encountered his old companion,
now Justice Shallow.*

SHALLOW O, Sir John, do you remember since we lay all night
in the Windmill in Saint George's Field?

SIR JOHN No more of that, good Master Shallow, no more of
that.

SHALLOW Ha, 'twas a merry night! And is Jane Nightwork
alive?

SIR JOHN She lives, Master Shallow.

SHALLOW She never could away with me.

SIR JOHN Never, never. She would always say she could not
abide Master Shallow.

SHALLOW By the mass, I could anger her to th' heart. She was
then a bona-roba. Doth she hold her own well?

SIR JOHN Old, old, Master Shallow.

SHALLOW Nay, she must be old; she cannot choose but be old;
certain she's old; and had Robin Nightwork by old Nightwork before I came to Clement's Inn.

SILENCE That's fifty-five year ago.

SHALLOW Ha, cousin Silence, that thou hadst seen that that
this knight and I have seen! Ha, Sir John, said I well?

SIR JOHN We have heard the chimes at midnight, Master
Shallow.

SHALLOW That we have, that we have; in faith, Sir John, we

have. Our watchword was 'Hem boys!' Come, let's to dinner; come, let's to dinner. Jesus, the days that we have seen! Come, come.

(2 *Henry IV*, 3.2.191–216)

A Winter Song

WINTER (*sings*)
    When icicles hang by the wall,
      And Dick the shepherd blows his nail,
    And Tom bears logs into the hall,
      And milk comes frozen home in pail;
    When blood is nipped, and ways be foul,
    Then nightly sings the staring owl:
    Tu-whit, tu-whoo!—a merry note,
    While greasy Joan doth keel the pot.

    When all aloud the wind doth blow,
      And coughing drowns the parson's saw,
    And birds sit brooding in the snow,
      And Marian's nose looks red and raw;
    When roasted crabs hiss in the bowl,
    Then nightly sings the staring owl:
    Tu-whit, tu-whoo!—a merry note,
    While greasy Joan doth keel the pot.
                  (*Love's Labour's Lost*, 5.2.898–913)

Places

The Forest of Ardenne

Duke Senior has been exiled.

DUKE SENIOR

 Now, my co-mates and brothers in exile,
 Hath not old custom made this life more sweet
 Than that of painted pomp? Are not these woods
 More free from peril than the envious court?
 Here feel we not the penalty of Adam,
 The seasons' difference, as the icy fang
 And churlish chiding of the winter's wind,
 Which when it bites and blows upon my body
 Even till I shrink with cold, I smile, and say
 'This is no flattery. These are counsellors
 That feelingly persuade me what I am.'
 Sweet are the uses of adversity
 Which, like the toad, ugly and venomous,
 Wears yet a precious jewel in his head;
 And this our life, exempt from public haunt,
 Finds tongues in trees, books in the running brooks,
 Sermons in stones, and good in everything.

AMIENS

 I would not change it. Happy is your grace
 That can translate the stubbornness of fortune
 Into so quiet and so sweet a style.

        (As You Like It, 2.1.1–20)

England Betrayed

Richard II's uncle, John of Gaunt, is disgusted that his nephew's
frivolous extravagance has made it necessary to lease out the land in
order to raise money for wars in Ireland.

JOHN OF GAUNT
    . . . This royal throne of kings, this sceptred isle,
    This earth of majesty, this seat of Mars,
    This other Eden, demi-paradise,
    This fortress built by nature for herself
    Against infection and the hand of war,
    This happy breed of men, this little world,
    This precious stone set in the silver sea,
    Which serves it in the office of a wall,
    Or as a moat defensive to a house
    Against the envy of less happier lands;
    This blessèd plot, this earth, this realm, this England,
    This nurse, this teeming womb of royal kings,
    Feared by their breed and famous by their birth,
    Renownèd for their deeds as far from home
    For Christian service and true chivalry
    As is the sepulchre, in stubborn Jewry,
    Of the world's ransom, blessèd Mary's son;
    This land of such dear souls, this dear dear land,
    Dear for her reputation through the world,
    Is now leased out—I die pronouncing it—

Like to a tenement or pelting farm.
England, bound in with the triumphant sea,
Whose rocky shore beats back the envious siege
Of wat'ry Neptune, is now bound in with shame,
With inky blots and rotten parchment bonds.
That England that was wont to conquer others
Hath made a shameful conquest of itself.
Ah, would the scandal vanish with my life,
How happy then were my ensuing death!

(Richard II, 2.1.40–68)

Dover Cliff

*The despairing Duke of Gloucester, cruelly blinded, has asked his son
Edgar, disguised as a beggar, to take him to a hilltop from which he can
throw himself.*

EDGAR

>Come on, sir, here's the place. Stand still. How fearful
>And dizzy 'tis to cast one's eyes so low!
>The crows and choughs that wing the midway air
>Show scarce so gross as beetles. Halfway down
>Hangs one that gathers samphire, dreadful trade!
>Methinks he seems no bigger than his head.
>The fishermen that walk upon the beach
>Appear like mice, and yon tall anchoring barque
>Diminished to her cock, her cock a buoy
>Almost too small for sight. The murmuring surge
>That on th'unnumbered idle pebble chafes
>Cannot be heard so high. I'll look no more,
>Lest my brain turn and the deficient sight
>Topple down headlong.

>>*(The Tragedy of King Lear, 4.5.11–24)*

A Woodland Bank

Oberon, King of the Fairies, speaks of a place where he will anoint his queen's eyes with magic juice.

OBERON

    . . . I know a bank where the wild thyme blows,
    Where oxlips and the nodding violet grows,
    Quite overcanopied with luscious woodbine,
    With sweet musk-roses, and with eglantine.
    There sleeps Titania sometime of the night,
    Lulled in these flowers with dances and delight;
    And there the snake throws her enamelled skin,
    Weed wide enough to wrap a fairy in.

        (A Midsummer Night's Dream, 2.1.249–56)

Stories

A Story of Birth and Death

Leontes, King of Sicily, believing his baby daughter to be begotten in adultery, has caused her to be abandoned on the coast of Bohemia by the courtier Antigonus, who has been chased and killed by a bear.

Enter an Old Shepherd

OLD SHEPHERD I would there were no age between ten and three-and-twenty, or that youth would sleep out the rest; for there is nothing in the between but getting wenches with child, wronging the ancientry, stealing, fighting—hark you now, would any but these boiled-brains of nineteen and two-and-twenty hunt this weather? They have scared away two of my best sheep, which I fear the wolf will sooner find than the master. If anywhere I have them, 'tis by the seaside, browsing of ivy. Good luck, an't be thy will!

He sees the babe

What have we here? Mercy on's, a bairn! A very pretty bairn. A boy or a child, I wonder? A pretty one, a very pretty one. Sure some scape. Though I am not bookish, yet I can read 'waiting-gentlewoman' in the scape. This has been some stair-work, some trunk-work, some behind-door-work. They were warmer that got this than the poor thing is here. I'll take it up for pity; yet I'll tarry till my son come. He hallooed but even now. Whoa-ho-hoa!

Enter Clown

CLOWN Hilloa, loa!

OLD SHEPHERD What, art so near? If thou'lt see a thing to talk
on when thou art dead and rotten, come hither. What ail'st
thou, man?

CLOWN I have seen two such sights, by sea and by land!
But I am not to say it is a sea, for it is now the sky.
Betwixt the firmament and it you cannot thrust a bodkin's
point.

OLD SHEPHERD Why, boy, how is it?

CLOWN I would you did but see how it chafes, how it rages, how
it takes up the shore. But that's not to the point. O, the most
piteous cry of the poor souls! Sometimes to see 'em, and not
to see 'em; now the ship boring the moon with her
mainmast, and anon swallowed with yeast and froth, as
you'd thrust a cork into a hogshead. And then for the land-
service, to see how the bear tore out his shoulder-bone, how
he cried to me for help, and said his name was Antigonus, a
nobleman! But to make an end of the ship—to see how the
sea flap-dragoned it! But first, how the poor souls roared,
and the sea mocked them, and how the poor gentleman
roared, and the bear mocked him, both roaring louder than
the sea or weather.

OLD SHEPHERD Name of mercy, when was this, boy?

CLOWN Now, now. I have not winked since I saw these sights.
The men are not yet cold under water, nor the bear half
dined on the gentleman. He's at it now.

OLD SHEPHERD Would I had been by to have helped the old
man!

CLOWN I would you had been by the ship side, to have helped her. There your charity would have lacked footing.

OLD SHEPHERD Heavy matters, heavy matters. But look thee here, boy. Now bless thyself. Thou metst with things dying, I with things new-born. Here's a sight for thee. Look thee, a bearing-cloth for a squire's child.

He points to the box

Look thee here, take up, take up, boy. Open't. So, let's see. It was told me I should be rich by the fairies. This is some changeling. Open't. What's within, boy?

CLOWN (*opening the box*) You're a made old man. If the sins of your youth are forgiven you, you're well to live. Gold, all gold!

OLD SHEPHERD This is fairy gold, boy, and 'twill prove so. Up with't, keep it close. Home, home, the next way. We are lucky, boy, and to be so still requires nothing but secrecy. Let my sheep go. Come, good boy, the next way home.

CLOWN Go you the next way with your findings. I'll go see if the bear be gone from the gentleman, and how much he hath eaten. They are never curst but when they are hungry. If there be any of him left, I'll bury it.

OLD SHEPHERD That's a good deed. If thou mayst discern by that which is left of him what he is, fetch me to th' sight of him.

CLOWN Marry will I; and you shall help to put him i'th' ground.

OLD SHEPHERD 'Tis a lucky day, boy, and we'll do good deeds on't.

(*The Winter's Tale*, 3.3.58–135)

A Tale as Tall as it is Long

The Duke of Ephesus has asked Egeon, a merchant of Syracuse, why he has risked death by landing illegally at Ephesus.

EGEON

　. . . In Syracusa was I born, and wed
Unto a woman happy but for me,
And by me happy, had not our hap been bad.
With her I lived in joy, our wealth increased
By prosperous voyages I often made
To Epidamnum, till my factor's death,
And the great care of goods at random left,
Drew me from kind embracements of my spouse,
From whom my absence was not six months old
Before herself—almost at fainting under
The pleasing punishment that women bear—
Had made provision for her following me,
And soon and safe arrivèd where I was.
There had she not been long but she became
A joyful mother of two goodly sons;
And, which was strange, the one so like the other
As could not be distinguished but by names.
That very hour, and in the selfsame inn,
A mean-born woman was deliverèd
Of such a burden male, twins both alike.
Those, for their parents were exceeding poor,

I bought, and brought up to attend my sons.
My wife, not meanly proud of two such boys,
Made daily motions for our home return.
Unwilling, I agreed. Alas! Too soon
We came aboard.
A league from Epidamnum had we sailed
Before the always-wind-obeying deep
Gave any tragic instance of our harm.
But longer did we not retain much hope,
For what obscurèd light the heavens did grant
Did but convey unto our fearful minds
A doubtful warrant of immediate death,
Which though myself would gladly have embraced,
Yet the incessant weepings of my wife—
Weeping before for what she saw must come—
And piteous plainings of the pretty babes,
That mourned for fashion, ignorant what to fear,
Forced me to seek delays for them and me.
And this it was—for other means was none:
The sailors sought for safety by our boat,
And left the ship, then sinking-ripe, to us.
My wife, more careful for the latter-born,
Had fastened him unto a small spare mast
Such as seafaring men provide for storms.
To him one of the other twins was bound,
Whilst I had been like heedful of the other.
The children thus disposed, my wife and I,
Fixing our eyes on whom our care was fixed,
Fastened ourselves at either end the mast,

And floating straight, obedient to the stream,
Was carried towards Corinth, as we thought.
At length the sun, gazing upon the earth,
Dispersed those vapours that offended us,
And by the benefit of his wishèd light
The seas waxed calm, and we discoverèd
Two ships from far, making amain to us:
Of Corinth that, of Epidaurus this.
But ere they came—O let me say no more!
Gather the sequel by that went before.

DUKE

Nay, forward, old man; do not break off so,
For we may pity though not pardon thee.

EGEON

O, had the gods done so, I had not now
Worthily termed them merciless to us.
For, ere the ships could meet by twice five leagues,
We were encountered by a mighty rock,
Which being violently borne upon,
Our helpful ship was splitted in the midst,
So that in this unjust divorce of us
Fortune had left to both of us alike
What to delight in, what to sorrow for.
Her part, poor soul, seeming as burdenèd
With lesser weight but not with lesser woe,
Was carried with more speed before the wind,
And in our sight they three were taken up
By fishermen of Corinth, as we thought.
At length another ship had seized on us,

And, knowing whom it was their hap to save,
Gave healthful welcome to their shipwrecked guests,
And would have reft the fishers of their prey
Had not their barque been very slow of sail;
And therefore homeward did they bend their course.
Thus have you heard me severed from my bliss,
That by misfortunes was my life prolonged
To tell sad stories of my own mishaps.

(The Comedy of Errors, 1.1.36–120)

Love-in-idleness

Titania, Queen of the Fairies, has refused to part with the changeling boy demanded by her husband Oberon (see p. 15); he tells Robin Goodfellow how he plans to bend her to his will.

OBERON

    . . . My gentle puck, come hither. Thou rememb'rest
    Since once I sat upon a promontory
    And heard a mermaid on a dolphin's back
    Uttering such dulcet and harmonious breath
    That the rude sea grew civil at her song
    And certain stars shot madly from their spheres
    To hear the sea-maid's music?

ROBIN   I remember.

OBERON

    That very time I saw, but thou couldst not,
    Flying between the cold moon and the earth
    Cupid, all armed. A certain aim he took
    At a fair vestal thronèd by the west,
    And loosed his love-shaft smartly from his bow
    As it should pierce a hundred thousand hearts.
    But I might see young Cupid's fiery shaft
    Quenched in the chaste beams of the wat'ry moon,
    And the imperial vot'ress passèd on,
    In maiden meditation, fancy-free.
    Yet marked I where the bolt of Cupid fell.

It fell upon a little western flower—
Before, milk-white; now, purple with love's wound—
And maidens call it love-in-idleness.
Fetch me that flower; the herb I showed thee once.
The juice of it on sleeping eyelids laid
Will make or man or woman madly dote
Upon the next live creature that it sees.
Fetch me this herb, and be thou here again
Ere the leviathan can swim a league.

ROBIN
I'll put a girdle round about the earth
In forty minutes.   *Exit*

OBERON   Having once this juice,
I'll watch Titania when she is asleep,
And drop the liquor of it in her eyes.
The next thing then she waking looks upon—
Be it on lion, bear, or wolf, or bull,
On meddling monkey, or on busy ape—
She shall pursue it with the soul of love.
And ere I take this charm from off her sight—
As I can take it with another herb—
I'll make her render up her page to me.

(A Midsummer Night's Dream, 2.1.148–85)

A Mischievous Tale

*At the command of Oberon, King of the Fairies, Robin Goodfellow has
dropped into Queen Titania's eyes the juice of love-in-idleness, causing
her to fall in love with Bottom the Weaver, on whom Robin has fixed
an ass's head.*

ROBIN

> My mistress with a monster is in love.
> Near to her close and consecrated bower
> While she was in her dull and sleeping hour
> A crew of patches, rude mechanicals
> That work for bread upon Athenian stalls,
> Were met together to rehearse a play
> Intended for great Theseus' nuptial day.
> The shallowest thickskin of that barren sort,
> Who Pyramus presented, in their sport
> Forsook his scene and entered in a brake,
> When I did him at this advantage take.
> An ass's nole I fixèd on his head.
> Anon his Thisbe must be answerèd,
> And forth my mimic comes. When they him spy—
> As wild geese that the creeping fowler eye,
> Or russet-pated choughs, many in sort,
> Rising and cawing at the gun's report,
> Sever themselves and madly sweep the sky—
> So, at his sight, away his fellows fly,

And at our stamp here o'er and o'er one falls.
He 'Murder' cries, and help from Athens calls.
Their sense thus weak, lost with their fears thus strong,
Made senseless things begin to do them wrong.
For briers and thorns at their apparel snatch;
Some sleeves, some hats—from yielders all things catch.
I led them on in this distracted fear,
And left sweet Pyramus translated there;
When in that moment, so it came to pass,
Titania waked and straightway loved an ass.

(*A Midsummer Night's Dream*, 3.2.6–34)

A Proposal of Marriage

Mistress Quickly, hostess of a tavern, has had Sir John Falstaff arrested for debt.

SIR JOHN *(to the Hostess)* What is the gross sum that I owe thee?

MISTRESS QUICKLY Marry, if thou wert an honest man, thyself, and the money too. Thou didst swear to me upon a parcel-gilt goblet, sitting in my Dolphin chamber, at the round table, by a sea-coal fire, upon Wednesday in Wheeson week, when the Prince broke thy head for liking his father to a singing-man of Windsor—thou didst swear to me then, as I was washing thy wound, to marry me, and make me my lady thy wife. Canst thou deny it? Did not goodwife Keech the butcher's wife come in then, and call me 'Gossip Quickly'—coming in to borrow a mess of vinegar, telling us she had a good dish of prawns, whereby thou didst desire to eat some, whereby I told thee they were ill for a green wound? And didst thou not, when she was gone downstairs, desire me to be no more so familiarity with such poor people, saying that ere long they should call me 'madam'? And didst thou not kiss me, and bid me fetch thee thirty shillings? I put thee now to thy book-oath; deny it if thou canst.

(2 Henry IV, 2.1.85–105)

A Fat Knight's Tale (1)

When Sir John Falstaff tried to seduce Mistress Ford, she tricked him into hiding in a laundry basket which she arranged to be emptied into the River Thames.

SIR JOHN ... Have I lived to be carried in a basket like a barrow of butcher's offal, and to be thrown in the Thames? Well, if I be served such another trick, I'll have my brains ta'en out and buttered, and give them to a dog for a New Year's gift. 'Sblood, the rogues slighted me into the river with as little remorse as they would have drowned a blind bitch's puppies, fifteen i'th' litter! And you may know by my size that I have a kind of alacrity in sinking. If the bottom were as deep as hell, I should down. I had been drowned, but that the shore was shelvy and shallow—a death that I abhor, for the water swells a man, and what a thing should I have been when I had been swelled? By the Lord, a mountain of mummy!

(The Merry Wives of Windsor, 3.5.4–17)

A Fat Knight's Tale (2)

Master Ford has disguised himself as Master Brooke; here Sir John Falstaff, not knowing Brooke's real identity, tells him of the trick that Mistress Ford had played.

SIR JOHN . . . As God would have it, comes in one Mistress Page, gives intelligence of Ford's approach, and, by her invention and Ford's wife's distraction, they conveyed me into a buck-basket—

FORD A buck-basket?

SIR JOHN By the Lord, a buck-basket!—rammed me in with foul shirts and smocks, socks, foul stockings, greasy napkins, that, Master Brooke, there was the rankest compound of villainous smell that ever offended nostril.

FORD And how long lay you there?

SIR JOHN Nay, you shall hear, Master Brooke, what I have suffered to bring this woman to evil, for your good. Being thus crammed in the basket, a couple of Ford's knaves, his hinds, were called forth by their mistress, to carry me, in the name of foul clothes, to Datchet Lane. They took me on their shoulders, met the jealous knave their master in the door, who asked them once or twice what they had in their basket. I quaked for fear lest the lunatic knave would have searched it, but fate, ordaining he should be a cuckold, held his hand. Well, on went he for a search, and away went I for foul clothes. But mark the sequel, Master Brooke. I suffered the pangs of three several deaths. First, an intolerable fright, to be detected with a jealous rotten bell-wether. Next, to be compassed like a good bilbo in the circumference of a peck, hilt to point, heel to head. And then, to be stopped in, like a strong distillation, with stinking clothes that fretted in their own grease. Think of that—a man of my kidney—think of that—that am as subject to heat as butter, a man of continual dissolution and thaw. It was a miracle to scape suffocation. And in the height of this bath, when I was more than half stewed in grease like a Dutch dish, to be thrown into the Thames and cooled, glowing-hot, in that surge, like a horseshoe. Think of that—hissing hot—think of that, Master Brooke!

(The Merry Wives of Windsor, 3.5.77–113)

The Murder of the Princes in the Tower

Richard III's nephews, the young Prince Edward and Richard, Duke of York, stand between him and the throne; he has bribed Sir James Tyrrell to kill them.

TYRRELL

> The tyrannous and bloody act is done—
> The most arch deed of piteous massacre
> That ever yet this land was guilty of.
> Dighton and Forrest, whom I did suborn
> To do this piece of ruthless butchery,
> Albeit they were fleshed villains, bloody dogs,
> Melted with tenderness and mild compassion,
> Wept like two children in their deaths' sad story.
> 'O thus', quoth Dighton, 'lay the gentle babes';
> 'Thus, thus', quoth Forrest, 'girdling one another
> Within their alabaster innocent arms.
> Their lips were four red roses on a stalk,
> And in their summer beauty kissed each other.
> A book of prayers on their pillow lay,
> Which once', quoth Forrest, 'almost changed my mind.
> But O, the devil'—there the villain stopped,
> When Dighton thus told on, 'We smotherèd
> The most replenishèd sweet work of nature,
> That from the prime creation e'er she framed.'
> Hence both are gone, with conscience and remorse.

They could not speak, and so I left them both,
To bear this tidings to the bloody king.

(Richard III, 4.3.1–22)

The New King and the Old

*Richard II has been deposed by Henry Bolingbroke; their aunt, the
Duchess of York, asks her husband to tell the story of their entry into
London.*

DUCHESS OF YORK

 My lord, you told me you would tell the rest,
 When weeping made you break the story off,
 Of our two cousins' coming into London.

YORK

 Where did I leave?

DUCHESS OF YORK At that sad stop, my lord,
 Where rude misgoverned hands from windows' tops
 Threw dust and rubbish on King Richard's head.

YORK

 Then, as I said, the Duke, great Bolingbroke,
 Mounted upon a hot and fiery steed,
 Which his aspiring rider seemed to know,
 With slow but stately pace kept on his course,
 Whilst all tongues cried 'God save thee, Bolingbroke!'
 You would have thought the very windows spake,
 So many greedy looks of young and old
 Through casements darted their desiring eyes
 Upon his visage, and that all the walls
 With painted imagery had said at once,
 'Jesu preserve thee! Welcome, Bolingbroke!'

Whilst he, from the one side to the other turning,
Bare-headed, lower than his proud steed's neck,
Bespake them thus: 'I thank you, countrymen',
And thus still doing, thus he passed along.

DUCHESS OF YORK

Alack, poor Richard! Where rode he the whilst?

YORK

As in a theatre the eyes of men,
After a well-graced actor leaves the stage,
Are idly bent on him that enters next,
Thinking his prattle to be tedious,
Even so, or with much more contempt, men's eyes
Did scowl on gentle Richard. No man cried 'God save
   him!'
No joyful tongue gave him his welcome home;
But dust was thrown upon his sacred head,
Which with such gentle sorrow he shook off,
His face still combating with tears and smiles,
The badges of his grief and patience,
That had not God for some strong purpose steeled
The hearts of men, they must perforce have melted,
And barbarism itself have pitied him.
But heaven hath a hand in these events,
To whose high will we bound our calm contents.
To Bolingbroke are we sworn subjects now,
Whose state and honour I for aye allow.

(Richard II, 5.2.1–40)

'Magic in the web . . .'

Planning to use Desdemona's handkerchief to arouse the jealousy of her husband, Othello, the villainous Iago has persuaded his wife, Desdemona's servant, to take it.

OTHELLO
    I have a salt and sorry rheum offends me.
    Lend me thy handkerchief.
DESDEMONA (*offering a handkerchief*) Here, my lord.
OTHELLO
    That which I gave you.
DESDEMONA   I have it not about me.
OTHELLO Not?
DESDEMONA
    No, faith, my lord.
OTHELLO   That's a fault. That handkerchief
    Did an Egyptian to my mother give.
    She was a charmer, and could almost read
    The thoughts of people. She told her, while she kept it
    'Twould make her amiable, and subdue my father
    Entirely to her love; but if she lost it,
    Or made a gift of it, my father's eye
    Should hold her loathèd, and his spirits should hunt
    After new fancies. She, dying, gave it me,
    And bid me, when my fate would have me wived,
    To give it her. I did so, and take heed on't.

Make it a darling, like your precious eye.
To lose't or give't away were such perdition
As nothing else could match.

DESDEMONA   Is't possible?

OTHELLO

'Tis true. There's magic in the web of it.
A sibyl that had numbered in the world
The sun to course two hundred compasses
In her prophetic fury sewed the work.
The worms were hallowed that did breed the silk,
And it was dyed in mummy, which the skilful
Conserved of maidens' hearts.

DESDEMONA   I'faith, is't true?

OTHELLO

Most veritable. Therefore look to't well.

(Othello, 3.4.51–76)

A Tale of Grief

*King Lear, who has disowned his youngest daughter Cordelia, has been
driven mad by the cruelty of his two elder daughters; Cordelia is now
Queen of France.*

KENT Did your letters pierce the Queen to any demonstration
　　　of grief?

FIRST GENTLEMAN

　　　Ay, sir. She took them, read them in my presence,
　　　And now and then an ample tear trilled down
　　　Her delicate cheek. It seemed she was a queen
　　　Over her passion who, most rebel-like,
　　　Sought to be king o'er her.

KENT　　　　　　　　　　　　　O, then it moved her.

FIRST GENTLEMAN

　　　Not to a rage. Patience and sorrow strove
　　　Who should express her goodliest. You have seen
　　　Sunshine and rain at once; her smiles and tears
　　　Were like, a better way. Those happy smilets
　　　That played on her ripe lip seemed not to know
　　　What guests were in her eyes, which parted thence
　　　As pearls from diamonds dropped. In brief,
　　　Sorrow would be a rarity most beloved
　　　If all could so become it.

KENT　　　　　　　　　　Made she no verbal question?

FIRST GENTLEMAN

　　　Faith, once or twice she heaved the name of 'father'

Pantingly forth as if it pressed her heart,
Cried 'Sisters, sisters, shame of ladies, sisters,
Kent, father, sisters, what, i'th' storm, i'th' night,
Let piety not be believed!' There she shook
The holy water from her heavenly eyes
And clamour mastered, then away she started
To deal with grief alone.

KENT   It is the stars,
The stars above us govern our conditions,
Else one self mate and make could not beget
Such different issues.

> (*The History of King Lear*, sc. 17, ll. 10–36)

A Father's Miseries

Edgar's father, the Duke of Gloucester, has had his eyes put out for supporting King Lear.

ALBANY

   . . . How have you known the miseries of your father?

EDGAR

By nursing them, my lord. List a brief tale,
And when 'tis told, O that my heart would burst!
The bloody proclamation to escape
That followed me so near—O, our lives' sweetness,
That we the pain of death would hourly die
Rather than die at once!—taught me to shift
Into a madman's rags, t'assume a semblance
That very dogs disdained; and in this habit
Met I my father with his bleeding rings,
Their precious stones new-lost; became his guide,
Led him, begged for him, saved him from despair;
Never—O fault!—revealed myself unto him
Until some half hour past, when I was armed.
Not sure, though hoping, of this good success,
I asked his blessing, and from first to last
Told him our pilgrimage; but his flawed heart—
Alack, too weak the conflict to support—
'Twixt two extremes of passion, joy and grief,
Burst smilingly.

(The Tragedy of King Lear, 5.3.172–91)

How a King Found his Heir

Leontes, King of Sicily, believing his daughter Perdita to be the illegitimate offspring of his queen Hermione and Polixenes, King of Bohemia, has ordered Antigonus, husband of Paulina, to abandon the baby on the shore of Bohemia (see pp. 299–301). Hermione had apparently died, but now, sixteen years later, Perdita is restored to her penitent father.

FIRST GENTLEMAN . . . The news, Ruggiero!

SECOND GENTLEMAN Nothing but bonfires. The oracle is fulfilled. The King's daughter is found. Such a deal of wonder is broken out within this hour, that ballad-makers cannot be able to express it.

    Enter another Gentleman

Here comes the Lady Paulina's steward. He can deliver you more.—How goes it now, sir? This news which is called true is so like an old tale that the verity of it is in strong suspicion. Has the King found his heir?

THIRD GENTLEMAN Most true, if ever truth were pregnant by circumstance. That which you hear you'll swear you see, there is such unity in the proofs. The mantle of Queen Hermione's, her jewel about the neck of it, the letters of Antigonus found with it, which they know to be his character; the majesty of the creature, in resemblance of the mother; the affection of nobleness which nature shows above her breeding, and many other evidences proclaim her with all certainty to be the King's daughter. Did you see the meeting of the two kings?

SECOND GENTLEMAN No.

THIRD GENTLEMAN Then have you lost a sight which was to be seen, cannot be spoken of. There might you have beheld one joy crown another, so and in such manner that it seemed sorrow wept to take leave of them, for their joy waded in tears. There was casting up of eyes, holding up of hands, with countenance of such distraction that they were to be known by garment, not by favour. Our king being ready to leap out of himself for joy of his found daughter, as if that joy were now become a loss cries, 'O, thy mother, thy mother!', then asks Bohemia forgiveness, then embraces his son-in-law, then again worries he his daughter with clipping her. Now he thanks the old shepherd, which stands by like a weather-bitten conduit of many kings' reigns. I never heard of such another encounter, which lames report to follow it, and undoes description to do it.

SECOND GENTLEMAN What, pray you, became of Antigonus, that carried hence the child?

THIRD GENTLEMAN Like an old tale still, which will have matter to rehearse though credit be asleep and not an ear open. He was torn to pieces with a bear. This avouches the shepherd's son, who has not only his innocence, which seems much, to justify him, but a handkerchief and rings of his, that Paulina knows.

FIRST GENTLEMAN What became of his barque and his followers?

THIRD GENTLEMAN Wrecked the same instant of their master's death, and in the view of the shepherd; so that all the instruments which aided to expose the child were even then lost when it was found. But O, the noble combat that 'twixt joy and sorrow was fought in Paulina! She had one eye declined for the loss of her husband, another elevated that the oracle was fulfilled. She lifted the Princess from the earth, and so locks her in embracing as if she would pin her to her heart, that she might no more be in danger of losing.

FIRST GENTLEMAN The dignity of this act was worth the audience of kings and princes, for by such was it acted.

THIRD GENTLEMAN One of the prettiest touches of all, and that which angled for mine eyes—caught the water, though not the fish—was when at the relation of the Queen's death, with the manner how she came to't bravely confessed and lamented by the King, how attentiveness wounded his daughter till from one sign of dolour to another she did, with an 'Alas', I would fain say bleed tears; for I am sure my heart wept blood. Who was most marble there changed colour. Some swooned, all sorrowed. If all the world could have seen't, the woe had been universal.

FIRST GENTLEMAN Are they returned to the court?

THIRD GENTLEMAN No. The Princess, hearing of her mother's statue, which is in the keeping of Paulina, a piece many years in doing, and now newly performed by that rare Italian master Giulio Romano, who, had he himself eternity and could put breath into his work, would beguile nature of her custom, so perfectly he is her ape. He so near to Hermione hath done Hermione that they say one would speak to her and stand in hope of answer. Thither with all

A Narrow Lane, an Old Man, and Two Boys

Posthumus, banished son-in-law of the British king Cymbeline, has arrived in Wales with the invading Roman army and disguised himself as a peasant so as not to have to fight against his own countrymen. Here he tells how, in battle, the day was saved for Britain by an unknown man and two youths—in fact Belarius and the King's two sons (see p. 10).

       Enter Posthumus like a poor soldier, and a Briton Lord

LORD

    Cam'st thou from where they made the stand?

POSTHUMUS   I did,

    Though you, it seems, come from the fliers.

LORD   Ay.

POSTHUMUS

    No blame be to you, sir, for all was lost,
    But that the heavens fought. The King himself
    Of his wings destitute, the army broken,
    And but the backs of Britons seen, all flying
    Through a strait lane; the enemy full-hearted,
    Lolling the tongue with slaught'ring, having work
    More plentiful than tools to do't, struck down
    Some mortally, some slightly touched, some falling
    Merely through fear, that the strait pass was dammed
    With dead men hurt behind, and cowards living
    To die with lengthened shame.

LORD   Where was this lane?

POSTHUMUS

> Close by the battle, ditched, and walled with turf;
> Which gave advantage to an ancient soldier,
> An honest one, I warrant, who deserved
> So long a breeding as his white beard came to,
> In doing this for 's country. Athwart the lane
> He with two striplings—lads more like to run
> The country base than to commit such slaughter;
> With faces fit for masks, or rather fairer
> Than those for preservation cased, or shame—
> Made good the passage, cried to those that fled
> 'Our Britain's harts die flying, not her men.
> To darkness fleet souls that fly backwards. Stand,
> Or we are Romans, and will give you that
> Like beasts which you shun beastly, and may save
> But to look back in frown. Stand, stand.' These three,
> Three thousand confident, in act as many—
> For three performers are the file when all
> The rest do nothing—with this word 'Stand, stand',
> Accommodated by the place, more charming
> With their own nobleness, which could have turned
> A distaff to a lance, gilded pale looks;
> Part shame, part spirit renewed, that some, turned
> > coward
> But by example—O, a sin in war,
> Damned in the first beginners!—gan to look
> The way that they did and to grin like lions
> Upon the pikes o'th' hunters. Then began

A stop i'th' chaser, a retire. Anon
A rout, confusion thick; forthwith they fly
Chickens the way which they stooped eagles; slaves,
The strides they victors made; and now our cowards,
Like fragments in hard voyages, became
The life o'th' need. Having found the back door open
Of the unguarded hearts, heavens, how they wound!
Some slain before, some dying, some their friends
O'erborne i'th' former wave, ten chased by one,
Are now each one the slaughterman of twenty.
Those that would die or ere resist are grown
The mortal bugs o'th' field.

LORD   This was strange chance:
A narrow lane, an old man, and two boys.

POSTHUMUS
Nay, do not wonder at it. Yet you are made
Rather to wonder at the things you hear
Than to work any. Will you rhyme upon't,
And vent it for a mock'ry? Here is one:
'Two boys, an old man twice a boy, a lane,
Preserved the Britons, was the Romans' bane.'

                              (*Cymbeline*, 5.5.1–58)

A Tale Untold

Petruccio's servant Grumio tells of his master's journey home with his bride, the shrewish Katherine.

GRUMIO . . . *Inprimis*, we came down a foul hill, my master riding behind my mistress.

CURTIS Both of one horse?

GRUMIO What's that to thee?

CURTIS Why, a horse.

GRUMIO Tell thou the tale. But hadst thou not crossed me thou shouldst have heard how her horse fell and she under her horse; thou shouldst have heard in how miry a place, how she was bemoiled, how he left her with the horse upon her, how he beat me because her horse stumbled, how she waded through the dirt to pluck him off me, how he swore, how she prayed that never prayed before, how I cried, how the horses ran away, how her bridle was burst, how I lost my crupper, with many things of worthy memory which now shall die in oblivion, and thou return unexperienced to thy grave.

(The Taming of the Shrew, 4.1.59–75)

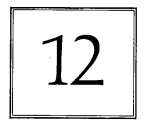

Death

The Sense of Death

Isabella is speaking to her brother Claudio, condemned to death for fornication.

ISABELLA

    . . . The sense of death is most in apprehension,
    And the poor beetle that we tread upon
    In corporal sufferance finds a pang as great
    As when a giant dies.

(Measure for Measure, 3.1.76–9)

Fearing Death

Having heard of prodigies in the streets (see pp. 218–19) on the eve of
the Ides of March, which her husband Julius Caesar has been told to
beware, Calpurnia has tried to deter him from leaving the house.

CAESAR

    Cowards die many times before their deaths;
    The valiant never taste of death but once.
    Of all the wonders that I yet have heard,
    It seems to me most strange that men should fear,
    Seeing that death, a necessary end,
    Will come when it will come.

(Julius Caesar, 2.2.32–7)

What We Fear of Death

Isabella has told her brother Claudio, condemned to death for fornication, that she could save his life by sleeping with Angelo, the Duke's deputy.

CLAUDIO Death is a fearful thing.
ISABELLA And shamèd life a hateful.
CLAUDIO
    Ay, but to die, and go we know not where;
    To lie in cold obstruction, and to rot;
    This sensible warm motion to become
    A kneaded clod, and the dilated spirit
    To bathe in fiery floods, or to reside
    In thrilling region of thick-ribbèd ice;
    To be imprisoned in the viewless winds,
    And blown with restless violence round about
    The pendent world; or to be worse than worst
    Of those that lawless and incertain thought
    Imagine howling—'tis too horrible!
    The weariest and most loathèd worldly life
    That age, ache, penury, and imprisonment
    Can lay on nature is a paradise
    To what we fear of death.

                (Measure for Measure, 3.1.116–32)

'What dreams may come . . .'

The ghost of Hamlet's father has told him to revenge his murder.

HAMLET

To be, or not to be; that is the question:
Whether 'tis nobler in the mind to suffer
The slings and arrows of outrageous fortune,
Or to take arms against a sea of troubles,
And, by opposing, end them. To die, to sleep—
No more, and by a sleep to say we end
The heartache and the thousand natural shocks
That flesh is heir to—'tis a consummation
Devoutly to be wished. To die, to sleep.
To sleep, perchance to dream. Ay, there's the rub,
For in that sleep of death what dreams may come
When we have shuffled off this mortal coil
Must give us pause. There's the respect
That makes calamity of so long life,
For who would bear the whips and scorns of time,
Th'oppressor's wrong, the proud man's contumely,
The pangs of disprized love, the law's delay,
The insolence of office, and the spurns
That patient merit of th'unworthy takes,
When he himself might his quietus make
With a bare bodkin? Who would these fardels bear,
To grunt and sweat under a weary life,

But that the dread of something after death,
The undiscovered country from whose bourn
No traveller returns, puzzles the will,
And makes us rather bear those ills we have
Than fly to others that we know not of?
Thus conscience does make cowards of us all,
And thus the native hue of resolution
Is sicklied o'er with the pale cast of thought,
And enterprises of great pith and moment
With this regard their currents turn awry,
And lose the name of action.

(Hamlet, 3.1.58–90)

A Dream of Drowning

George, Duke of Clarence (imprisoned in the Tower of London by his brother King Edward IV as the result of plotting by his other brother, the future Richard III), tells his keeper Brackenbury of a dream that, drowning, he was confronted with the spirits of those he had wronged.

CLARENCE

    . . . O Lord! Methought what pain it was to drown,
    What dreadful noise of waters in my ears,
    What sights of ugly death within my eyes.
    Methoughts I saw a thousand fearful wrecks,
    Ten thousand men that fishes gnawed upon,
    Wedges of gold, great ouches, heaps of pearl,
    Inestimable stones, unvalued jewels,
    All scattered in the bottom of the sea.
    Some lay in dead men's skulls; and in those holes
    Where eyes did once inhabit, there were crept—
    As 'twere in scorn of eyes—reflecting gems,
    Which wooed the slimy bottom of the deep
    And mocked the dead bones that lay scattered by.

BRACKENBURY

    Had you such leisure in the time of death,
    To gaze upon these secrets of the deep?

CLARENCE

    Methought I had, and often did I strive
    To yield the ghost, but still the envious flood

Stopped-in my soul and would not let it forth
To find the empty, vast, and wand'ring air,
But smothered it within my panting bulk,
Who almost burst to belch it in the sea.

BRACKENBURY

Awaked you not in this sore agony?

CLARENCE

No, no, my dream was lengthened after life.
O then began the tempest to my soul!
I passed, methought, the melancholy flood,
With that sour ferryman which poets write of,
Unto the kingdom of perpetual night.
The first that there did greet my stranger soul
Was my great father-in-law, renownèd Warwick,
Who cried aloud, 'What scourge for perjury
Can this dark monarchy afford false Clarence?'
And so he vanished. Then came wand'ring by
A shadow like an angel, with bright hair,
Dabbled in blood, and he shrieked out aloud,
'Clarence is come: false, fleeting, perjured Clarence,
That stabbed me in the field by Tewkesbury.
Seize on him, furies! Take him unto torment!'
With that, methoughts a legion of foul fiends
Environed me, and howlèd in mine ears
Such hideous cries that with the very noise
I trembling waked, and for a season after
Could not believe but that I was in hell,
Such terrible impression made my dream.

(Richard III, 1.4.21–63)

339

Dusty Death

*The usurper Macbeth, besieged by the opposing Scottish and English
forces, hears that his wife has died.*

SEYTON

    The Queen, my lord, is dead.

MACBETH   She should have died hereafter.

    There would have been a time for such a word.
    Tomorrow, and tomorrow, and tomorrow
    Creeps in this petty pace from day to day
    To the last syllable of recorded time,
    And all our yesterdays have lighted fools
    The way to dusty death. Out, out, brief candle.
    Life's but a walking shadow, a poor player
    That struts and frets his hour upon the stage,
    And then is heard no more. It is a tale
    Told by an idiot, full of sound and fury,
    Signifying nothing.

(Macbeth, 5.5.16–27)

Last Words

The aged and ailing John of Gaunt has been advised not to waste his breath in attempting to give good advice to his wayward nephew, Richard II.

JOHN OF GAUNT

    O, but they say the tongues of dying men
    Enforce attention, like deep harmony.
    Where words are scarce they are seldom spent in vain,
    For they breathe truth that breathe their words in pain.
    He that no more must say is listened more
       Than they whom youth and ease have taught to
          glose.
    More are men's ends marked than their lives before.
       The setting sun, and music at the close,
    As the last taste of sweets, is sweetest last,
    Writ in remembrance more than things long past.
    Though Richard my life's counsel would not hear,
    My death's sad tale may yet undeaf his ear.

                  (Richard II, 2.1.5–16)

A Last Message

Timon had exiled himself from Athens in bitter disillusionment; now, Athenian senators have begged him to return and lead their army against Alcibiades, another exile whose campaign Timon has supported.

TIMON

    Come not to me again, but say to Athens,
    Timon hath made his everlasting mansion
    Upon the beachèd verge of the salt flood,
    Who once a day with his embossèd froth
    The turbulent surge shall cover. Thither come,
    And let my gravestone be your oracle.
    Lips, let four words go by, and language end.
    What is amiss, plague and infection mend.
    Graves only be men's works, and death their gain.
    Sun, hide thy beams. Timon hath done his reign.

Exit into his cave

(*Timon of Athens*, 5.2.99–108)

The Death of Kings

Richard II's supporters are deserting him and flocking to his enemy
Henry Bolingbroke, who has executed Richard's favourites and is
advancing towards a confrontation.

KING RICHARD
    . . . For God's sake, let us sit upon the ground,
    And tell sad stories of the death of kings—
    How some have been deposed, some slain in war,
    Some haunted by the ghosts they have deposed,
    Some poisoned by their wives, some sleeping killed,
    All murdered. For within the hollow crown
    That rounds the mortal temples of a king
    Keeps Death his court; and there the antic sits,
    Scoffing his state and grinning at his pomp,
    Allowing him a breath, a little scene,
    To monarchize, be feared, and kill with looks,
    Infusing him with self and vain conceit,
    As if this flesh which walls about our life
    Were brass impregnable; and humoured thus,
    Comes at the last, and with a little pin
    Bores through his castle wall; and farewell, king.
                    (Richard II, 3.2.151–66)

A Death in Childbed, at Sea

Pericles Prince of Tyre is at sea with his wife Thaisa, who is expecting their first child.

Thunder and lightning. Enter Pericles a-shipboard

PERICLES

> The god of this great vast rebuke these surges
> Which wash both heav'n and hell; and thou that hast
> Upon the winds command, bind them in brass,
> Having called them from the deep. O still
> Thy deaf'ning dreadful thunders, gently quench
> Thy nimble sulph'rous flashes.—O, ho, Lychorida!
> How does my queen?—Thou stormest venomously.
> Wilt thou spit all thyself? The seaman's whistle
> Is as a whisper in the ears of death,
> Unheard.—Lychorida!—Lucina, O!
> Divinest patroness, and midwife gentle
> To those that cry by night, convey thy deity
> Aboard our dancing boat, make swift the pangs
> Of my queen's travails!—Now, Lychorida.
>
> *Enter Lychorida with an infant*

LYCHORIDA

> Here is a thing too young for such a place,
> Who, if it had conceit, would die, as I
> Am like to do. Take in your arms this piece
> Of your dead queen.

PERICLES   How, how, Lychorida?

LYCHORIDA

    Patience, good sir, do not assist the storm.
    Here's all that is left living of your queen,
    A little daughter. For the sake of it
    Be manly, and take comfort.

PERICLES   O you gods!

    Why do you make us love your goodly gifts,
    And snatch them straight away? We here below
    Recall not what we give, and therein may
    Use honour with you.

LYCHORIDA   Patience, good sir,
    E'en for this charge.

> *She gives him the infant. Pericles, looking mournfully*
> *upon it, shakes his head, and weeps*

PERICLES   Now mild may be thy life,

    For a more blust'rous birth had never babe;
    Quiet and gentle thy conditions, for
    Thou art the rudeliest welcome to this world
    That e'er was prince's child; happy what follows.
    Thou hast as chiding a nativity
    As fire, air, water, earth, and heav'n can make
    To herald thee from th' womb. Poor inch of nature,
    Ev'n at the first thy loss is more than can
    Thy partage quit with all thou canst find here.
    Now the good gods throw their best eyes upon't.

> *Enter the Master and a Sailor*

MASTER What, courage, sir! God save you.

PERICLES

>That's but your superstition.

>It hath done to me its worst. Yet for the love

>Of this poor infant, this fresh new seafarer,

>I would it would be quiet.

MASTER *(calling)* Slack the bow-lines, there.—Thou wilt not, wilt thou? Blow, and split thyself.

SAILOR But searoom, an the brine and cloudy billow kiss the moon, I care not.

MASTER *(to Pericles)* Sir, your queen must overboard. The sea works high, the wind is loud, and will not lie till the ship be cleared of the dead.

PERICLES

>That's but your superstition.

MASTER Pardon us, sir; with us at sea it hath been still observed, and we are strong in custom. Therefore briefly yield 'er, for she must overboard straight.

PERICLES

>As you think meet. Most wretched queen!

LYCHORIDA   Here she lies, sir.

>>*She draws the curtains and discovers the body of Thaisa*
>>*in a bed. Pericles gives Lychorida the infant*

PERICLES *(to Thaisa)*

>A terrible childbed hast thou had, my dear,

>No light, no fire. Th'unfriendly elements

>Forgot thee utterly, nor have I time

>To give thee hallowed to thy grave, but straight

>Must cast thee, scarcely coffined, in the ooze,

>Where, for a monument upon thy bones

And aye-remaining lamps, the belching whale
And humming water must o'erwhelm thy corpse,
Lying with simple shells.

(*Pericles*, sc. 11, ll. 1–63)

Death by Poison

The French army, led by the Dauphin, has invaded England. King John, who—as Philip Falconbridge, the Bastard, knows—has been poisoned by a monk, is with his nobles and his son, Prince Henry.

PRINCE HENRY . . . 'Tis strange that death should sing.
 I am the cygnet to this pale faint swan,
 Who chants a doleful hymn to his own death,
 And from the organ-pipe of frailty sings
 His soul and body to their lasting rest.
SALISBURY
 Be of good comfort, Prince, for you are born
 To set a form upon that indigest
 Which he hath left so shapeless and so rude.
  King John is brought in
KING JOHN
 Ay marry, now my soul hath elbow-room;
 It would not out at windows nor at doors.
 There is so hot a summer in my bosom
 That all my bowels crumble up to dust;
 I am a scribbled form, drawn with a pen
 Upon a parchment, and against this fire
 Do I shrink up.
PRINCE HENRY How fares your majesty?
KING JOHN
 Poisoned, ill fare! Dead, forsook, cast off;

And none of you will bid the winter come
To thrust his icy fingers in my maw,
Nor let my kingdom's rivers take their course
Through my burned bosom, nor entreat the north
To make his bleak winds kiss my parchèd lips
And comfort me with cold. I do not ask you much;
I beg cold comfort, and you are so strait
And so ingrateful you deny me that.

PRINCE HENRY

O, that there were some virtue in my tears
That might relieve you!

KING JOHN   The salt in them is hot.
Within me is a hell, and there the poison
Is, as a fiend, confined to tyrannize
On unreprievable condemnèd blood.

Enter the Bastard

BASTARD

O, I am scalded with my violent motion
And spleen of speed to see your majesty!

KING JOHN

O cousin, thou art come to set mine eye.
The tackle of my heart is cracked and burnt,
And all the shrouds wherewith my life should sail
Are turnèd to one thread, one little hair;
My heart hath one poor string to stay it by,
Which holds but till thy news be utterèd,
And then all this thou seest is but a clod
And module of confounded royalty.

BASTARD

> The Dauphin is preparing hitherward,
> Where God He knows how we shall answer him;
> For in a night the best part of my power,
> As I upon advantage did remove,
> Were in the Washes all unwarily
> Devourèd by the unexpected flood.
>
> *King John dies*

SALISBURY

> You breathe these dead news in as dead an ear.
> (*To King John*) My liege, my lord!—But now a king, now
> thus.

PRINCE HENRY

> Even so must I run on, and even so stop.
> What surety of the world, what hope, what stay,
> When this was now a king and now is clay?

> > > (*King John*, 5.7.20–69)

Death of a Comrade

Sir John Falstaff's former cronies have had news of his death.

PISTOL   . . . Bardolph,
> Be blithe; Nim, rouse thy vaunting veins; boy, bristle
> Thy courage up. For Falstaff he is dead,
> And we must earn therefore.

BARDOLPH Would I were with him, wheresome'er he is, either in heaven or in hell.

HOSTESS Nay, sure he's not in hell. He's in Arthur's bosom, if ever man went to Arthur's bosom. A made a finer end, and went away an it had been any christom child. A parted ev'n just between twelve and one, ev'n at the turning o'th' tide—for after I saw him fumble with the sheets, and play with flowers, and smile upon his finger's end, I knew there was but one way. For his nose was as sharp as a pen, and a babbled of green fields. 'How now, Sir John?' quoth I. 'What, man! Be o' good cheer.' So a cried out, 'God, God, God', three or four times. Now I, to comfort him, bid him a should not think of God; I hoped there was no need to trouble himself with any such thoughts yet. So a bade me lay more clothes on his feet. I put my hand into the bed and felt them, and they were as cold as any stone. Then I felt to his knees, and so up'ard and up'ard, and all was as cold as any stone.

NIM They say he cried out of sack.

HOSTESS Ay, that a did.

BARDOLPH And of women.

HOSTESS Nay, that a did not.

BOY Yes, that a did, and said they were devils incarnate.

HOSTESS A could never abide carnation, 'twas a colour he never liked.

BOY A said once the devil would have him about women.

HOSTESS A did in some sort, indeed, handle women—but then he was rheumatic, and talked of the Whore of Babylon.

BOY Do you not remember, a saw a flea stick upon Bardolph's nose, and a said it was a black soul burning in hell-fire.

BARDOLPH Well, the fuel is gone that maintained that fire. That's all the riches I got in his service.

(Henry V, 2.3.3–41)

A Death by Water

Laertes' sister Ophelia has gone mad after her former lover Hamlet has killed their father Polonius, believing him to be Claudius, murderer of Hamlet's father and second husband of Hamlet's mother, Gertrude.

QUEEN GERTRUDE

One woe doth tread upon another's heel,
So fast they follow. Your sister's drowned, Laertes.

LAERTES Drowned? O, where?

QUEEN GERTRUDE

There is a willow grows aslant a brook
That shows his hoar leaves in the glassy stream.
Therewith fantastic garlands did she make
Of crow-flowers, nettles, daisies, and long purples,
That liberal shepherds give a grosser name,
But our cold maids do dead men's fingers call them.
There on the pendent boughs her crownet weeds
Clamb'ring to hang, an envious sliver broke,
When down the weedy trophies and herself
Fell in the weeping brook. Her clothes spread wide,
And mermaid-like a while they bore her up;
Which time she chanted snatches of old tunes,
As one incapable of her own distress,
Or like a creature native and endued
Unto that element. But long it could not be

Till that her garments, heavy with their drink,
Pulled the poor wretch from her melodious lay
To muddy death.

(Hamlet, 4.7.135–55)

A Queen's Death

Cleopatra's lover Mark Antony has killed himself; now she too com-
mits suicide, so as to avoid being taken prisoner and led in triumph by
Octavius Caesar.

CLEOPATRA

Give me my robe. Put on my crown. I have
Immortal longings in me. Now no more
The juice of Egypt's grape shall moist this lip.
    Charmian and Iras help her to dress
Yare, yare, good Iras, quick—methinks I hear
Antony call. I see him rouse himself
To praise my noble act. I hear him mock
The luck of Caesar, which the gods give men
To excuse their after wrath. Husband, I come.
Now to that name my courage prove my title.
I am fire and air; my other elements
I give to baser life. So, have you done?
Come then, and take the last warmth of my lips.
    She kisses them
Farewell, kind Charmian. Iras, long farewell.
    Iras falls and dies
Have I the aspic in my lips? Dost fall?
If thou and nature can so gently part,
The stroke of death is as a lover's pinch,
Which hurts and is desired. Dost thou lie still?

If thus thou vanishest, thou tell'st the world
It is not worth leave-taking.

CHARMIAN

Dissolve, thick cloud, and rain, that I may say
The gods themselves do weep.

CLEOPATRA   This proves me base.
If she first meet the curlèd Antony
He'll make demand of her, and spend that kiss
Which is my heaven to have.

She takes an aspic from the basket and puts it to her breast

Come, thou mortal wretch,
With thy sharp teeth this knot intrinsicate
Of life at once untie. Poor venomous fool,
Be angry, and dispatch. O, couldst thou speak,
That I might hear thee call great Caesar ass
Unpolicied!

CHARMIAN   O eastern star!

CLEOPATRA   Peace, peace.
Dost thou not see my baby at my breast,
That sucks the nurse asleep?

CHARMIAN   O, break! O, break!

CLEOPATRA

As sweet as balm, as soft as air, as gentle.
O Antony!

She puts another aspic to her arm
Nay, I will take thee too.

What should I stay—   *She dies*

CHARMIAN   In this vile world? So, fare thee well.

Now boast thee, death, in thy possession lies
A lass unparalleled. Downy windows, close,
And golden Phoebus never be beheld
Of eyes again so royal.

(*Antony and Cleopatra*, 5.2.275–312)

A Noble Death

King Duncan's son Malcolm reports on the execution of the treacherous Thane of Cawdor.

MALCOLM   . . . Nothing in his life
    Became him like the leaving it. He died
    As one that had been studied in his death
    To throw away the dearest thing he owed
    As 'twere a careless trifle.   .

                                (*Macbeth*, 1.4.7–11)

Lament of a Goddess

*Having escaped the importunate advances of Venus, goddess of love,
the mortal youth Adonis has been slain in a boar-hunt.*

'Alas, poor world, what treasure hast thou lost,
What face remains alive that's worth the viewing?
Whose tongue is music now? What canst thou boast
Of things long since, or anything ensuing?
  The flowers are sweet, their colours fresh and trim;
  But true sweet beauty lived and died with him.

'Bonnet nor veil henceforth no creature wear:
Nor sun nor wind will ever strive to kiss you.
Having no fair to lose, you need not fear.
The sun doth scorn you, and the wind doth hiss you.
  But when Adonis lived, sun and sharp air
  Lurked like two thieves to rob him of his fair;

'And therefore would he put his bonnet on,
Under whose brim the gaudy sun would peep.
The wind would blow it off, and, being gone,
Play with his locks; then would Adonis weep,
  And straight, in pity of his tender years,
  They both would strive who first should dry his tears.

'To see his face the lion walked along
Behind some hedge, because he would not fear him.
To recreate himself when he hath sung,
The tiger would be tame, and gently hear him.
  If he had spoke, the wolf would leave his prey,
  And never fright the silly lamb that day.

'When he beheld his shadow in the brook,
The fishes spread on it their golden gills.
When he was by, the birds such pleasure took
That some would sing, some other in their bills
  Would bring him mulberries and ripe-red cherries.
  He fed them with his sight, they him with berries.

'But this foul, grim, and urchin-snouted boar,
Whose downward eye still looketh for a grave,
Ne'er saw the beauteous livery that he wore:
Witness the entertainment that he gave.
  If he did see his face, why then, I know
  He thought to kiss him, and hath killed him so.

''Tis true, 'tis true; thus was Adonis slain;
He ran upon the boar with his sharp spear,
Who did not whet his teeth at him again,
But by a kiss thought to persuade him there,
  And, nuzzling in his flank, the loving swine
  Sheathed unaware the tusk in his soft groin.

'Had I been toothed like him, I must confess
With kissing him I should have killed him first;
But he is dead, and never did he bless
My youth with his, the more am I accursed.'
  With this she falleth in the place she stood,
  And stains her face with his congealèd blood.

She looks upon his lips, and they are pale.
She takes him by the hand, and that is cold.
She whispers in his ears a heavy tale,
As if they heard the woeful words she told.
  She lifts the coffer-lids that close his eyes,
  Where lo, two lamps burnt out in darkness lies;

Two glasses, where herself herself beheld
A thousand times, and now no more reflect,
Their virtue lost, wherein they late excelled,
And every beauty robbed of his effect.
  'Wonder of time,' quoth she, 'this is my spite,
  That, thou being dead, the day should yet be light.'
                    (*Venus and Adonis*, 1075–1134)

A Scene of Mourning

The princess Innogen, journeying through Wales disguised as a man, took refuge with Belarius and the two men Guiderius and Arviragus, whom he has brought up as his sons but who in reality are her brothers (see p. 10). Guiderius has just beheaded the villainous Cloten, and Innogen has taken a potion which creates in her the outward appearance of death.

Solemn music

BELARIUS   My ingenious instrument!—
    Hark, Polydore, it sounds. But what occasion
    Hath Cadwal now to give it motion? Hark!

GUIDERIUS
    Is he at home?

BELARIUS   He went hence even now.

GUIDERIUS
    What does he mean? Since death of my dear'st mother
    It did not speak before. All solemn things
    Should answer solemn accidents. The matter?
    Triumphs for nothing and lamenting toys
    Is jollity for apes and grief for boys.
    Is Cadwal mad?

        Enter from the cave Arviragus with Innogen, dead,
        bearing her in his arms

BELARIUS   Look, here he comes,
    And brings the dire occasion in his arms
    Of what we blame him for.

ARVIRAGUS   . The bird is dead
    That we have made so much on. I had rather
    Have skipped from sixteen years of age to sixty,
    To have turned my leaping time into a crutch,
    Than have seen this.

GUIDERIUS (*to Innogen*)   O sweetest, fairest lily!
    My brother wears thee not one half so well
    As when thou grew'st thyself.

BELARIUS   O melancholy,
    Who ever yet could sound thy bottom, find
    The ooze to show what coast thy sluggish crare
    Might easiliest harbour in? Thou blessèd thing,
    Jove knows what man thou mightst have made; but I,
    Thou diedst a most rare boy, of melancholy.
    (*To Arviragus*) How found you him?

ARVIRAGUS   Stark, as you see,
    Thus smiling as some fly had tickled slumber,
    Not as death's dart being laughed at; his right cheek
    Reposing on a cushion.

GUIDERIUS   Where?

ARVIRAGUS   O'th' floor,
    His arms thus leagued. I thought he slept, and put
    My clouted brogues from off my feet, whose rudeness
    Answered my steps too loud.

GUIDERIUS   Why, he but sleeps.
    If he be gone he'll make his grave a bed.
    With female fairies will his tomb be haunted,
    (*To Innogen*) And worms will not come to thee.

ARVIRAGUS (*to Innogen*)   With fairest flowers

Whilst summer lasts and I live here, Fidele,
I'll sweeten thy sad grave. Thou shalt not lack
The flower that's like thy face, pale primrose, nor
The azured harebell, like thy veins; no, nor
The leaf of eglantine, whom not to slander
Outsweetened not thy breath. The ruddock would
With charitable bill—O bill sore shaming
Those rich-left heirs that let their fathers lie
Without a monument!—bring thee all this,
Yea, and furred moss besides, when flowers are none,
To winter-gown thy corpse.

GUIDERIUS   Prithee, have done,
And do not play in wench-like words with that
Which is so serious. Let us bury him,
And not protract with admiration what
Is now due debt. To th' grave.

ARVIRAGUS   Say, where shall 's lay him?

GUIDERIUS

By good Euriphile, our mother.

ARVIRAGUS   Be't so,
And let us, Polydore, though now our voices
Have got the mannish crack, sing him to th' ground
As once our mother; use like note and words,
Save that 'Euriphile' must be 'Fidele'.

GUIDERIUS Cadwal,
I cannot sing. I'll weep, and word it with thee,
For notes of sorrow out of tune are worse
Than priests and fanes that lie.

ARVIRAGUS   We'll speak it then.

BELARIUS

    Great griefs, I see, medicine the less, for Cloten
    Is quite forgot. He was a queen's son, boys,
    And though he came our enemy, remember
    He was paid for that. Though mean and mighty rotting
    Together have one dust, yet reverence,
    That angel of the world, doth make distinction
    Of place 'tween high and low. Our foe was princely,
    And though you took his life as being our foe,
    Yet bury him as a prince.

GUIDERIUS   Pray you, fetch him hither.
    Thersites' body is as good as Ajax'
    When neither are alive.

ARVIRAGUS *(to Belarius)*   If you'll go fetch him,
    We'll say our song the whilst.   *Exit Belarius*

                    Brother, begin.

GUIDERIUS

    Nay, Cadwal, we must lay his head to th'east.
    My father hath a reason for't.

ARVIRAGUS   'Tis true.

GUIDERIUS

    Come on, then, and remove him.

ARVIRAGUS   So, begin.

GUIDERIUS

       Fear no more the heat o'th' sun,
         Nor the furious winter's rages.
       Thou thy worldly task hast done,
         Home art gone and ta'en thy wages.

> Golden lads and girls all must,
> As chimney-sweepers, come to dust.

ARVIRAGUS

> Fear no more the frown o'th' great,
>   Thou art past the tyrant's stroke.
> Care no more to clothe and eat,
>   To thee the reed is as the oak.
> The sceptre, learning, physic, must
> All follow this and come to dust.

GUIDERIUS

> Fear no more the lightning flash,

ARVIRAGUS   Nor th'all-dreaded thunder-stone.

GUIDERIUS

> Fear not slander, censure rash.

ARVIRAGUS   Thou hast finished joy and moan.

GUIDERIUS *and* ARVIRAGUS

> All lovers young, all lovers must
> Consign to thee and come to dust.

GUIDERIUS

> No exorcisor harm thee,

ARVIRAGUS

> Nor no witchcraft charm thee.

GUIDERIUS

> Ghost unlaid forbear thee.

ARVIRAGUS

> Nothing ill come near thee.

GUIDERIUS *and* ARVIRAGUS

> Quiet consummation have,
> And renownèd be thy grave.

Enter Belarius with the body of Cloten in Posthumus'
suit

GUIDERIUS

We have done our obsequies. Come, lay him down.

BELARIUS

Here's a few flowers, but 'bout midnight more;
The herbs that have on them cold dew o'th' night
Are strewings fitt'st for graves upon th'earth's face.
You were as flowers, now withered; even so
These herblets shall, which we upon you strow.
Come on, away; apart upon our knees
[   ]
The ground that gave them first has them again.
Their pleasures here are past, so is their pain.

(*Cymbeline*, 4.2.187–292)

A Funeral Oration

*Mark Antony speaks over the body of Julius Caesar, assassinated by
Brutus and his fellow-conspirators.*

ANTONY

    Friends, Romans, countrymen, lend me your ears.
    I come to bury Caesar, not to praise him.
    The evil that men do lives after them;
    The good is oft interrèd with their bones.
    So let it be with Caesar. The noble Brutus
    Hath told you Caesar was ambitious.
    If it were so, it was a grievous fault,
    And grievously hath Caesar answered it.
    Here, under leave of Brutus and the rest—
    For Brutus is an honourable man,
    So are they all, all honourable men—
    Come I to speak in Caesar's funeral.
    He was my friend, faithful and just to me.
    But Brutus says he was ambitious,
    And Brutus is an honourable man.
    He hath brought many captives home to Rome,
    Whose ransoms did the general coffers fill.
    Did this in Caesar seem ambitious?
    When that the poor have cried, Caesar hath wept.
    Ambition should be made of sterner stuff.
    Yet Brutus says he was ambitious,

And Brutus is an honourable man.
You all did see that on the Lupercal
I thrice presented him a kingly crown,
Which he did thrice refuse. Was this ambition?
Yet Brutus says he was ambitious,
And sure he is an honourable man.
I speak not to disprove what Brutus spoke,
But here I am to speak what I do know.
You all did love him once, not without cause.
What cause withholds you then to mourn for him?
O judgement, thou art fled to brutish beasts,
And men have lost their reason!

  He weeps

          Bear with me.
My heart is in the coffin there with Caesar,
And I must pause till it come back to me.

        (Julius Caesar, 3.2.74–108)

Meditation on a Skull

*Hamlet, Prince of Denmark, and his friend Horatio watch a labourer
prepare a grave which (though they do not know it) is intended for the
body of Ophelia (see pp. 353–4).*

FIRST CLOWN ... Here's a skull, now. This skull has lain in the
    earth three and twenty years.

HAMLET Whose was it?

FIRST CLOWN A whoreson mad fellow's it was. Whose do you
    think it was?

HAMLET Nay, I know not.

FIRST CLOWN A pestilence on him for a mad rogue—a poured a
    flagon of Rhenish on my head once! This same skull, sir,
    was Yorick's skull, the King's jester.

HAMLET This?

FIRST CLOWN E'en that.

HAMLET Let me see.

    He takes the skull

    Alas, poor Yorick. I knew him, Horatio—a fellow of infinite
jest, of most excellent fancy. He hath borne me on his back a
thousand times; and now, how abhorred my imagination
is! My gorge rises at it. Here hung those lips that I have
kissed I know not how oft. Where be your gibes now, your
gambols, your songs, your flashes of merriment that were
wont to set the table on a roar? Not one now to mock your
own grinning? Quite chop-fallen? Now get you to my

lady's chamber and tell her, let her paint an inch thick, to this favour she must come. Make her laugh at that.

(*Hamlet*, 5.1.168–90)

Death in Battle Averted

Sir John Oldcastle (whose name Shakespeare changed, under pressure from the historical character's descendants, to Falstaff) encounters his old friend Prince Harry (later Henry V) at the Battle of Shrewsbury.

SIR JOHN Hal, if thou see me down in the battle, and bestride me, so. 'Tis a point of friendship.

PRINCE HARRY Nothing but a colossus can do thee that friendship. Say thy prayers, and farewell.

SIR JOHN I would 'twere bed-time, Hal, and all well.

PRINCE HARRY Why, thou owest God a death.   *Exit*

SIR JOHN 'Tis not due yet. I would be loath to pay him before his day. What need I be so forward with him that calls not on me? Well, 'tis no matter; honour pricks me on. Yea, but how if honour prick me off when I come on? How then? Can honour set-to a leg? No. Or an arm? No. Or take away the grief of a wound? No. Honour hath no skill in surgery, then? No. What is honour? A word. What is in that word 'honour'? What is that 'honour'? Air. A trim reckoning! Who hath it? He that died o' Wednesday. Doth he feel it? No. Doth he hear it? No. 'Tis insensible then? Yea, to the dead. But will it not live with the living? No. Why? Detraction will not suffer it. Therefore I'll none of it. Honour is a mere scutcheon. And so ends my catechism.

(1 Henry IV, 5.1.121–40)

Mourning Forbidden

No longer mourn for me when I am dead
Than you shall hear the surly sullen bell
Give warning to the world that I am fled
From this vile world with vilest worms to dwell.
Nay, if you read this line, remember not
The hand that writ it; for I love you so
That I in your sweet thoughts would be forgot
If thinking on me then should make you woe.
O, if, I say, you look upon this verse
When I perhaps compounded am with clay,
Do not so much as my poor name rehearse,
But let your love even with my life decay,
  Lest the wise world should look into your moan
  And mock you with me after I am gone.

(Sonnet 71)

'The readiness is all'

Hamlet, Prince of Denmark, who is to fight a duel with Laertes, has felt forebodings, but rejects Horatio's offer to postpone the duel.

HAMLET . . . There's a special providence in the fall of a sparrow. If it be now, 'tis not to come. If it be not to come, it will be now. If it be not now, yet it will come. The readiness is all. Since no man has aught of what he leaves, what is't to leave betimes?

(Hamlet, 5.2.165–70)

A Consolation against Death

Claudio, condemned to death for fornication, has expressed fear of death (see p. 335); the Duke of Vienna, disguised as a friar, counsels him.

DUKE

> Be absolute for death. Either death or life
> Shall thereby be the sweeter. Reason thus with life.
> If I do lose thee, I do lose a thing
> That none but fools would keep. A breath thou art,
> Servile to all the skyey influences
> That dost this habitation where thou keep'st
> Hourly afflict. Merely thou art death's fool,
> For him thou labour'st by thy flight to shun,
> And yet runn'st toward him still. Thou art not noble,
> For all th'accommodations that thou bear'st
> Are nursed by baseness. Thou'rt by no means valiant,
> For thou dost fear the soft and tender fork
> Of a poor worm. Thy best of rest is sleep,
> And that thou oft provok'st, yet grossly fear'st
> Thy death, which is no more. Thou art not thyself,
> For thou exist'st on many a thousand grains
> That issue out of dust. Happy thou art not,
> For what thou hast not, still thou striv'st to get,
> And what thou hast, forget'st. Thou art not certain,
> For thy complexion shifts to strange effects

After the moon. If thou art rich, thou'rt poor,
For like an ass whose back with ingots bows,
Thou bear'st thy heavy riches but a journey,
And death unloads thee. Friend hast thou none,
For thine own bowels, which do call thee sire,
The mere effusion of thy proper loins,
Do curse the gout, serpigo, and the rheum,
For ending thee no sooner. Thou hast nor youth nor
   age,
But as it were an after-dinner's sleep
Dreaming on both; for all thy blessèd youth
Becomes as agèd, and doth beg the alms
Of palsied eld; and when thou art old and rich,
Thou hast neither heat, affection, limb, nor beaüty,
To make thy riches pleasant. What's in this
That bears the name of life? Yet in this life
Lie hid more thousand deaths; yet death we fear
That makes these odds all even.

CLAUDIO   I humbly thank you.
To sue to live, I find I seek to die,
And seeking death, find life. Let it come on.

(Measure for Measure, 3.1.5–44)

Death Conquered

Poor soul, the centre of my sinful earth,
[   ] these rebel powers that thee array;
Why dost thou pine within and suffer dearth,
Painting thy outward walls so costly gay?
Why so large cost, having so short a lease,
Dost thou upon thy fading mansion spend?
Shall worms, inheritors of this excess,
Eat up thy charge? Is this thy body's end?
Then, soul, live thou upon thy servant's loss,
And let that pine to aggravate thy store.
Buy terms divine in selling hours of dross;
Within be fed, without be rich no more.
  So shalt thou feed on death, that feeds on men,
  And death once dead, there's no more dying then.

(Sonnet 146)

Unconsidered Trifles

LEAR (*removing his crown of weeds*)
    When we are born, we cry that we are come
    To this great stage of fools.

                            (*The Tragedy of King Lear*, 4.5.178–9)

❁

JAQUES Rosalind is your love's name?
ORLANDO Yes, just.
JAQUES I do not like her name.
ORLANDO There was no thought of pleasing you when she was
    christened.

                            (*As You Like It*, 3.2.258–62)

❁

CLAUDIO Silence is the perfectest herald of joy.

                        (*Much Ado About Nothing*, 2.1.287)

❁

ORLANDO O, how bitter a thing it is to look into happiness
    through another man's eyes.

                          (*As You Like It*, 5.2.41–2)

O father, what a hell of witchcraft lies
In the small orb of one particular tear!

('A Lover's Complaint', 288–9)

❁

ROSALIND Do you not know I am a woman? When I think, I
must speak.

(*As You Like It*, 3.2.244–5)

❁

FESTE Many a good hanging prevents a bad marriage.

(*Twelfth Night*, 1.5.18)

❁

BIONDELLO I knew a wench married in an afternoon as she
went to the garden for parsley to stuff a rabbit, and so may
you, sir, and so adieu, sir.

(*The Taming of the Shrew*, 4.5.25–7)

❁

TOUCHSTONE The truest poetry is the most feigning.

(*As You Like It*, 3.3.16–17)

❁

BENEDICK Is it not strange that sheep's guts should hale souls
out of men's bodies?

(*Much Ado About Nothing*, 2.3.57–9)

PRINCE HARRY

    If all the year were playing holidays,
    To sport would be as tedious as to work.

(1 Henry IV, 1.2.201–2)

❀

SIR TOBY I am sure care's an enemy to life.

(Twelfth Night, 1.3.2)

❀

ROSALINE

    A jest's prosperity lies in the ear
    Of him that hears it, never in the tongue
    Of him that makes it.

(Love's Labour's Lost, 5.2.848–50)

❀

LEONATO How much better is it to weep at joy than to joy at
    weeping!

(Much Ado About Nothing, 1.1.27–8)

❀

SIR JOHN FALSTAFF O, you shall see him laugh till his face be
    like a wet cloak ill laid up!

(2 Henry IV, 5.1.76–7)

CURTIS Who is that calls so coldly?

GRUMIO A piece of ice. If thou doubt it, thou mayst slide from my shoulder to my heel with no greater a run but my head and my neck.

(The Taming of the Shrew, 4.1.11–14)

❁

ISABELLA

O, it is excellent
To have a giant's strength, but it is tyrannous
To use it like a giant.

(Measure for Measure, 2.2.109–11)

❁

MENENIUS There is no more mercy in him than there is milk in a male tiger.

(Coriolanus, 5.4.28–9)

❁

ARMADO I am ill at reckoning; it fitteth the spirit of a tapster.

(Love's Labour's Lost, 1.2.40–1)

❁

BISHOP OF CARLISLE

My lord, wise men ne'er wail their present woes,
But presently prevent the ways to wail.

(Richard II, 3.2.174–5)

CLEOPATRA

Celerity is never more admired
Than by the negligent.

(Antony and Cleopatra, 3.7.24–5)

❁

CAPTAIN

What great ones do the less will prattle of.

(Twelfth Night, 1.2.29)

❁

DROMIO OF SYRACUSE

'Fly pride' says the peacock.

(The Comedy of Errors, 4.3.80)

❁

KING JOHN

How oft the sight of means to do ill deeds
Make deeds ill done!

(King John, 4.2.220–1)

❁

FLAMINIUS

Has friendship such a faint and milky heart
It turns in less than two nights?

(Timon of Athens, 2.2.53–4)

IAGO

> Trifles light as air
> Are to the jealous confirmations strong
> As proofs of holy writ.

(Othello, 3.3.326–8)

❀

FIRST LORD DUMAINE The web of our life is of a mingled
yarn, good and ill together. Our virtues would be proud if
our faults whipped them not, and our crimes would despair
if they were not cherished by our virtues.

(All's Well That Ends Well, 4.3.74–7)

❀

GREMIO

> And may not young men die as well as old?

(The Taming of the Shrew, 2.1.387)

❀

TIMON

> My long sickness
> Of health and living now begins to mend,
> And nothing brings me all things.

(Timon of Athens, 5.2.71–3)

❀

EDGAR

> Men must endure
> Their going hence even as their coming hither.

(The Tragedy of King Lear, 5.2.9–10)

A SELECT GLOSSARY

a, he (unemphatic form)
accommodations, conveniences, comforts
accomplish, equip perfectly
accoutred, armed
adventure, at, by chance, at random
adventures, at all, at all events, whatever came of it
affection, disposition
affections, emotions, inclinations
affray, frighten
affront, (v.) confront, balance
aggravate, increase
Alcides, Hercules
ambuscado, ambush
an, if
angel, gold coin worth from a third to half of a pound
antic, buffoon, jester
antre, cave
ape, imitator
arbitrament, arbitration
Argus, a hundred-eyed, mythical monster
arras, hanging
atomi, tiny beings
attaint, weakness, exhaustion
Aurora, the dawn

bake, cake together
ban, (n.) curse
bane, (v.) poison
barbed, with flanks protected by armour

barm, yeast, froth
base, prisoner's base (a children's game)
basilisk, legendary reptile said to kill by breath and look
bate, reduce
bate, (in falconry) beat the wings
batlet, wooden bat, paddle for washing clothes
bavin, brushwood
bearing-cloth, christening robe
beldame, grandmother
bell-wether, leading sheep of a flock, cuckold
bemoiled, covered with mud
beteem, grant, afford
bilbo, well-tempered sword (bent into a circle to test its strength)
bob, taunt, quip
bodkin, needle
bona-roba, high-class prostitute, courtesan
book, by the, according to the rules, with proper formality
boot, use, avail; booty
bootless, useless, unavailing; fruitlessly
bottom, keel, hull; ship
bourn, boundary
brave, fine
buck-basket, laundry basket
buffet, fight

caitiff, wretched, base

can, knows
carded, mixed, contaminated
carrack, large trading vessel, galleon
carve, show courtesy, make affected
　gestures
cased, covered, masked
casque, helmet
casualties, awkward, adverse
　happenings
character, handwriting
charmer, sorcerer
check at, be diverted by
child, baby girl
christom child, a baby in its
　christening cloth
cinque-spotted, having five spots
cipher, zero
circumstance, details
clip, embrace
clouted, hobnailed
clown, rustic
cock-pit, enclosed space used for
　cock-fights
codpiece, flap on the breeches worn
　before the genitals
coil, to-do, fuss
collied, dark, coal-black
comparative, one who invents
　(satirical) comparisons
complexion, constitution, bodily
　make-up
composture, manure, compost
conceit, power of thought
confounded, wasted, worn away
congreeing, agreeing, according
congreet, meet amicably
continent, border, shore
controversy, hearts of, hearts that
　contend courageously
cope withal, come into contact with

cot, cote, cottage
coulter, blade in front of a
　ploughshare
counterpoise, match
crab, crabapple
crank, winding path or course
crare, small trading vessel
crudy, 'curdy', thick
crupper, saddle-strap
curst, ill-tempered, shrewish
Cynthia, the moon-goddess
Cytherea, Venus, goddess of love

Dardanian, Trojan
deliver, unburden myself
deracinate, uproot
derogate, debased
diffused, disordered
Dis, god of the underworld
discover, reveal, disclose
disprized, held in contempt
distemperature, illness
distinction, discrimination
divers, varied
division, florid melody
doit, coin of slight value, trifle
dole, lot, destiny
doubtful, fearful
drave, drove
drawer, tapster, barman
drive, drove
ducat, European gold coin of
　variable value
dump, mournful tune or song

ean, bring forth lambs
earn, grieve
effusion, that which is poured out,
　offspring
egg, something of little value; *take*

eggs for money accept injury tamely
Egyptian, gypsy
eld, old age
element, sky
elf-locks, tangled mass of hair
ell, measure of length, about 30 cm
embossed, swollen
emportment, the state of being carried away by passion
enfeoff, hand over, surrender
envy, malice, hatred
equal, fair, impartial
Erebus, classical personification of darkness, gloomy region of the Underworld
erne, grieve
erst, once, formerly
estate, condition
even-plashed, evenly interwoven

fain, obliged
fair, (n.) beauty
fane, temple
farced, stuffed, padded pompously out
fardel, burden
farthingale, hooped petticoat
favour, face, appearance
fet, fetched
field, battlefield
flaw, squall, storm
fleshed, experienced
flexure, bowing, bending
flood, river, sea
forgetive, creative, inventive
form, formality, ceremony
fret, decay
fretten, chafed, blasted
front, brow

froward, perverse, awkward

galled, fretted (with salt water)
gaud, plaything
gender, offspring
gentle, (v.) ennoble
get, beget
given, disposed
glassy, frail as glass
glaze, stare, glare
glose, flatter, talk smoothly
gossip, gossiping, tattling woman
green-sickness, anaemia common mainly in young women

haggard, wild female hawk
hanging, genital development
hautboy, wind instrument, ancestor of the oboe
head, army
Hecate, goddess of the moon and of night
Hiems, winter personified
high-lone, quite alone, without support
hind, servant
his, its
history, story
holidam, 'halidom', holiness, virtue
home, speak, do justice
hood, (in falconry) blindfold
host, army
hunt's-up, an early-morning song
husbandry, produce
Hyperion, sun god

imbecility, weakness
immured, walled up
imperator, absolute ruler
incapable, unaware

inch-meal, by, little by little
indigest, formless mess
infixture, stability
inherit, put (one) in possession of
inprimis, in the first place
intentively, intently
intrinsicate, intricate, entangled
it, its

jaunce, (n.) trudging about
jauncing, trudging

kecksies, dry hollow stems
keel, (v.) prevent (a pot) from
    boiling over by stirring,
    skimming, etc.
keep, inhabit, stay within

lade, empty
leagued, crossed
let, (n.) hindrance
linstock, staff used to ignite
    gunpowder in a cannon
look what, whatever
Lucina, goddess of childbirth
lurch, cheat, rob

main, main part; *main flood* high
    tide
mainly, entirely
make, (n.) spouse
marry, indeed, to be sure
maw, belly
mean, middle part
meanly, poorly, badly
mechanic, labouring
mechanical, labourer
meed, reward
mend, improve upon
mere, absolute
mess, portion

mimic, burlesque actor, mime
mistress, sweetheart
modern, commonplace, trite
module, mere image or counterfeit
momentany, momentary
moral, (v.) moralize
mortally, humanly
mow, make faces, grimace
mummy, dead flesh
muniments, protectors
murrain, diseased

next, nearest, shortest
noble, gold coin worth a third of a
    pound
nole, head
numbers, verses

o'erhanging, canopy
office, (v.) act as a servant
officed, appointed to an office,
    having a particular function
operance, operation
ordinary, meal
orthography, orthographer, verbal
    pedant
ouches, gems, jewels
owe, own

parcels, by, piecemeal
parcel-gilt, partly gilded
pard, panther or leopard
pardie, by God, indeed
paritor, court official
parmacity, spermaceti
partage, freight, cargo
paten, thin metal plate
peck, round vessel used to measure
    a peck
Phaëton, son of Phoebus, permitted

to drive the chariot of the sun for
one disastrous day
Phoebus, the sun god
piece, (v.) augment
pill, plunder, rob
plantage, plants (supposed to
increase as the moon waxes)
plays, games, sports
point-device, extremely precise
poke, pocket
portage, portholes
portance, behaviour
pouncet-box, small box for
perfumes
precurrer, forerunner
presence, royal presence-chamber
present, immediate
presently, immediately
prime, spring
private, (n.) one not holding a
public position
prodigious, abnormal, monstrous
Proserpina, daughter of Ceres, the
goddess of agriculture
puck, mischievous spirit, goblin
puling, whining(ly)
push, attack

quern, handmill
quotidian, quotidian fever
(recurring daily)

ravin, ravenous
receipt, that which is received
rehearsal, recital
remember, recall
reremice, bats
Rhenish, German wine
rheum, catarrh
riggish, licentious

rivage, shore
rood, Cross
roundel, round dance
rub, obstacle
ruddock, robin redbreast
rude, rough, uncultivated

sable, black
sad, serious, solemn
sans, without
scape, escapade
scutcheon, hatchment of arms
displaying the armorial bearings
of a deceased person
seely, innocent, simple
sensible, sensitive
serpigo, skin disease
several, separate
shrewd, mischievous
silly, innocent, harmless
simples, herbs
sir-reverence, (corruption) save
your reverence
slight, (v.) toss contemptuously
Sol, the sun
sort, rank, kind
spinner, spider
squash, unripe pea-pod
still, continually
still-piecing, constantly closing itself
up again
stint, stop
stomach, appetite, inclination;
proud spirit
stone, testicle
straight, straight away, immediately
strait, niggardly, close; narrow

table, notebook
tables, backgammon

tall, brave
Tereus, in classical legend, the rapist of Philomela
thick, (of sight) dim
threne, threnody, dirge
thrift, gain, profit
thwart, perverse
tissue, cloth woven from gold thread and silk
toy, ornament, trinket
treble-dated, living three times as long as man
treis-puissant, thrice-powerful
trill, trickle
trow, believe, think
turtle, turtle-dove

unmanned, (in falconry) not accustomed to man
unpolicied, unskilled in the conduct of public affairs .
unquestionable, untalkative, taciturn

urchin-shows, visions of goblins
urchin-snouted, having a snout like a hedgehog

vail, lower
Vice, a character in old morality plays, commonly represented with a dagger
videlicet, that is to say, namely
vot'ress, woman under a vow
voucher, witness, testament

want, lack
watch, stay up late
waxen, increase, grow louder
Wheeson, Whitsun
wight, person
wink, close
wit, intelligence
worm, tick, mite (breeding in the hand)
wot, know

INDEX